Feminists, Pornography, & the Law

Feminists, Pornography, & the Law

*An Annotated Bibliography
of Conflict, 1970–1986*

Betty-Carol Sellen
Patricia A. Young

Library Professional Publications
1987

First published 1987 as a Library Professional Publication,
an imprint of The Shoe String Press, Inc.,
Hamden, Connecticut 06514
Printed in the United States of America

Set in Galliard by Coghill Composition Co.,
Richmond, Virginia
Designed by Patricia Larsen

Library of Congress Cataloging-in-Publication Data

Sellen, Betty–Carol.
    Feminists pornography & the law.

    Includes index.
    1. Pornography—Social aspects—United States—
Bibliography. 2. Feminism—United States—Bibliography.
3. Censorship—United States—Bibliography. 4. Obscenity
—(Law)—United States—Bibliography. I. Young,Patricia
A. II. Title. III. Title: Feminists pornography
and the law.
Z7164.P84S45   1987   [HQ471]   016.3634'7   87-2915
    ISBN 0-208-02124-8

Contents

Acknowledgments

The authors would like to thank the many people who helped with the bibliography by recommending sources, sending information, and suggesting leads to material. Of special significance was the assistance of the following people: Sue Searing, Women's Studies Librarian at the University of Wisconsin; Ellen Broidy, University of California, Irvine, Library; Andy Garoogian, Brooklyn College Library; Jody Bush, Berkeley Public Library; Kathryn Phenix, Denver Public Library; Mary Creixall-Vela, Houston Public Library; Jacquelyn Marie, University of California, Santa Cruz, Library; Christine Jenkins; Neil Parikh, San Francisco Public Library; and Cynthia Johanson of the Library of Congress. Barbara Scheele of the Brooklyn College Library and Rosemarie Riechel of Queens Borough Public Library helped us with their computer-based searches. William Parise and Rita Coleman of the Brooklyn College Interlibrary Loan service provided us with resources from all over the country. Judith Cormier and Ruth Colker led us to feminist lawyers. Joan Nestle of the Lesbian Herstory Archives supplied impressive resources and kind assistance. Dorice Horne, Brooklyn College Library, offered technical advice and Bernice Clegg did the hard part on the "PC", adding drama to the project by her exclaiming, from time to time, "I think I just lost the whole thing."

Introduction

In the 1970s, with the resurgence of the feminist movement, the conflict over pornography took a new turn. Women began to organize to protest pornography, because it was seen to be sexist and often degrading to women, showing them as stupid objects being manipulated for men's pleasure. As the decade progressed so did the pornography industry, providing billions to its owners and producers. And, to the observer, the pornography became more and more violent, the link pornographers made between sex and violence, more obvious.

The traditional liberal perspective on pornography is that it is harmless, perhaps even serving as a safety valve to keep males from acting out violent fantasies. Further, there is the conviction that nothing about it is dangerous enough to risk tampering with First Amendment freedoms—which are believed to protect pornography. An alternative view—that of many feminists—is that pornography reinforces the subordination of women and leads to actual violence against them. As for their view of the freedom of speech issue, it can best be summed up by a quote from Susan Brownmiller: "Nowhere is it written that you can exploit a woman's body because of the First Amendment."[1]

Conflicts and concern over freedom of speech versus restrictions on sexually explicit materials have a long history. The U.S. Government has sponsored several studies on obscenity, pornography, and their affect on people's lives.[2] The report of President Lyndon Johnson's Commission on Obscenity and Pornography (1970) stirred up controversy. The majority opinion was that the commission found no evidence for the belief that exposure to sexually explicit materials resulted in any harm to people. Several commission members protested this conclusion and filed a minority report. Since then, there have been other studies critical of the commission, charging that the research was faulty and reflected male bias.[3]

Early protests against pornography took the form of education about pornography and civil disobedience. In 1976 feminists protested a billboard promoting the Rolling Stones which pictured a battered, barely dressed woman with the caption, "I'm Black and

Blue from the Rolling Stones and I Love It." Two years later a cover of *Hustler* magazine featured a woman being ground up in a meat grinder to illustrate publisher Larry Flynt's promise, "We will no longer hang women up like pieces of meat." Feminists were not amused.

Soon after this there began the slide shows, demonstrations, and marches through "porn strips." In November 1978, the first national conference on pornography, "Feminist Perspectives on Pornography," was held in San Francisco. Organized by Women Against Violence in Pornography and Media, it protested violence in pornography and the use of violent pornographic images of women in media in order to sell products. In 1979 Women Against Pornography was organized in New York City and began its consciousness-raising activities. Since then, more organizations have been formed throughout the United States and in Canada to protest pornography as violence against women. "Take Back the Night" marches have taken place in many cities to protest pornography and other manifestations of violence toward women.

Acts of civil disobedience have also been used against pornographers and those who sell or distribute their products: Media Watch, Preying Mantis, and other groups have come up with a variety of direct actions. In Canada, the Wimmin's Fire Brigade took credit for trashing some video stores.

In the 1980s Andrea Dworkin and Catharine MacKinnon wrote an ordinance, introduced in Minneapolis and then in a number of other cities, which they hoped would provide a legislative solution to the problem of pornography. After Minneapolis in 1983, the ordinance was introduced in Indianapolis in 1984; Los Angeles in June 1985; Suffolk County, New York in December 1984; and, in November 1985, in Cambridge, Massachusetts. This antipornography law defined pornography as sex discrimination and those damaged by it as having been denied their civil rights. The introduction of the proposed law accelerated a divisiveness already beginning among feminists. Opposition to the law came from civil libertarians who suggested the ordinance conflicted with the First Amendment, from those who believed feminist publications would be endangered, and from those who doubted that the elimination of pornography would have anything to do with eliminating violence against women.

The 1982 Barnard Conference in New York (The Scholar and the Feminist: Toward a Politics of Sexuality) provided a scene of confrontation between feminists determined to fight pornography and those who believed the fight would limit women's rights to explore all kinds of sexuality. Mary Kay Blakcly called attention to this aspect of the conflict by using, as the title of her April 1985 *Ms* article, "Is One Woman's Sexuality Another Woman's Pornography?"

The Feminist Anti-Censorship Task Force (FACT) was organized to fight the Dworkin-MacKinnon ordinance and to show that not all feminists shared the same perception of the antipornography movement. FACT filed a friend-of-the-court brief on 10 April 1985 in federal appeals court asking that the Indianapolis ordinance be declared unconstitutional.

On 24 February 1986 the Indianapolis law that would have defined pornography as sex discrimination and made porn producers, distributors, and exhibitors subject to civil lawsuits was ruled unconstitutional by the U.S. Supreme Court. The justices delivered their decision without opinion, upholding lower court rulings that the Indianapolis statute interfered with free speech. Just as this book was being completed, U.S. Attorney General Meese and his Commission on Pornography issued their final report, and various antipornography groups promised to accelerate their direct actions against pornographers.

This bibliography is a guide to materials on the antipornography debate. This debate has been growing and shifting in emphasis over the last ten years. In addition to published materials, it includes unpublished reports, nonprint materials and relevant organizations. It does not include citations to legal cases nor does it, with two or three exceptions, include reports of the research done on the link between viewing pornography and committing acts of violence. Publications listed are from 1970, when there were very few, to late 1986.

References were retrieved from several computer-accessed data bases and from many standard, printed periodical indexes and newspaper indexes. Every book and article located led to many more, found in the footnotes, references, and bibliographies. The publications of the Women's Studies Librarian-at-Large at the University of Wisconsin (Madison), Sue Searing, and the rich collections of the Lesbian Herstory Archives in New York City were valuable sources. The most valuable resource of all has been the network of knowledgeable feminist librarians throughout the country.

The authors of this bibliography, whatever their private feelings and personal commitments, took a neutral stand in preparing this book. Although the bibliography is selective in terms of quantity of items, all positions in the antipornography debate are represented. If there is a preponderance of material on one side or another, it reflects only the quantity of publications produced by the various antagonists. The annotations quote the material cited and qualitative judgments—whether of the writing or the contents—were withheld.

This bibliography has been prepared to help people form a thoughtful, active response to the complicated issues of equality for women, sexual freedom, and the preservation of free speech.

Notes

1. Susan Brownmiller quoted by Georgia Dullea, "In Feminist's Antipornography Drive, 42nd Street Is the Target." *New York Times*, 6 July 1979, sec. A, 12.

2. U.S. Commission on Obscenity and Pornography. *Technical Report of the Commission on Obscenity and Pornography*. 10 vols. Washington: Government Printing Office, 1971.
   U.S. Commission on Obscenity and Pornography. *Report of the Commission on Obscenity and Pornography*. Washington: Government Printing Office, 1970.
   U.S. National Commission on the Causes and Prevention of Violence. *To Establish Justice, to Ensure Domestic Tranquility*. Final report of the National Commission on the Causes and Prevention of Violence. Washington: Government Printing Office, 1969.
   U.S. Public Health Service. Surgeon General. *Television and Growing Up: The Impact of Televised Violence*. Report to the Surgeon General from the Surgeon General's Scientific Advisory Committee on Television and Social Behavior. Washington: Government Printing Office, 1972.

3. An essay which deals critically with the commission's methodology is Irene Diamond's "Pornography and Repression: A Reconsideration," in *The Criminal Justice System and Women*, edited by Barbara Price and Natalie Sokoloff. This is listed here in the section on books. See also the article by Caryn Jacobs, "Patterns of Violence: A Feminist Perspective on the Regulation of Pornography," *Harvard Women's Law Journal* 7, Spring 1984, in the magazine section of this bibliography.

Abbreviations

ABC   American Broadcasting Company

ACLU   American Civil Liberties Union

ALA   American Library Association

CBS   Columbia Broadcasting System

COYOTE   Call Off Your Old Tired Ethics

E.R.A.   Equal Rights Amendment

FACT   Feminist Anti-Censorship Task Force

FAP   Feminists Against Pornography

FCC   Federal Communications Commission

GCN   *Gay Community News*

MIT   Massachusetts Institute of Technology

NBC   National Broadcasting Company

NCAC   National Coalition Against Censorship

NOW   National Organization for Women

NYLA   New York Library Association

NYU   New York University

SIECUS   Sex Information and Education Council of the United States

S/M, S & M   Sadomasochism

UCLA   University of Southern California at Los Angeles

WAAP   Women's Alliance Against Pornography

W.A.G.E.   Women's Alliance to Gain Equality

WAP   Women Against Pornography

WAVPM   Women Against Violence in Pornography and Media

1.
Books

This section of the bibliography lists and annotates books published from 1970 to late 1986. It includes works that in some way link feminists and pornography. These can be a woman's view of pornography and what it means in our culture, such as Susan Griffin's *Pornography and Silence: Culture's Revenge Against Nature,* or a consideration of pornography as evidence of men's oppression of women in such books as Andrea Dworkin's *Pornography: Men Possessing Women* and Laura Lederer's collection, *Take Back the Night: Women on Pornography.* Other books listed are critical of the feminist antipornography point of view; for example, *Women, Sex and Pornography: A Controversial and Unique Study* by Beatrice Faust, or the *Caught Looking: Feminism, Pornography & Censorship* published by FACT.

Excluded from the list are the many theoretical and philosophical books on issues of free speech and pornography in general. These works are easy to locate in standard indexes. The bibliography by Byerly and Rubin cited here is a useful starting place for finding material on pornography. Legal works and scientific research reports are excluded from this list with a few exceptions: three research reports mentioned frequently are included. These are by Hans Eysenck, Dolf Zimmerman, and Edward Donnerstein.

A Space Collective. *Issues of Censorship.* Toronto: Our Times
    Publishing Co., 1985.
    A Space is a collectively run artists' center in Toronto. On 31 May 1984 the Ontario Censor Board seized video tapes and equipment—an action that was subsequently overturned. This *Issues of Censorship* was a project sparked by that raid. Content includes writing by Varda Burstyn, "Struggling For Our Own Voices: Censorship and Self-Censorship," "Porn/Censor Wars and the Battlefield of Sex" by Gary Kinsman, and many more.

Alderfer, Hannah, Beth Jaker, and Marybeth Nelson. *Diary of a Conference on Sexuality*. Record of the Planning Committee of the Conference The Scholar and the Feminist IX: Toward a Politics of Sexuality. New York: Barnard College Women's Center, 1982.

The Ninth Annual Scholar and Feminist Conference at Barnard in 1982 was to become notorious because of the confrontation between those who "offered papers and workshops by more than forty feminists who represented a wide range of positions on the question of sexuality" and their opponents who objected to their emphasis on the "unorthodox." The "hard-line view that pornography supports patriarchy was not represented." Women Against Pornography and many others were very angry about the point of view presented. This publication is a record of what went into the planning of this conference.

Atwood, Margaret. *The Handmaid's Tale*. Boston: Houghton Mifflin Co., 1986.

A novel in which a new society is forecast, one that comes about, in part, because of feminist "excesses" in the present society. Among other things liberality toward pornography in the courts, in the media, and on the newsstand is blamed for the resulting social victory of the right-wing forces. The narrator blames her mother's burning of pornographic magazines as an influence for bringing about the new and oppressive society. Mary McCarthy in her review of this book (*New York Times Book Review*, 9 February 1986, 1, 35) says that Atwood fails to make her case in an otherwise readable book.

Barry, Kathleen. *Female Sexual Slavery*. Englewood Cliffs, N. J.: Prentice–Hall, 1979.

In the chapter entitled "Pornography: The Ideology of Cultural Sadism," the author describes prominent themes in pornography, the effects of the pornographic experience, the role of pornography in cultural sadism, and the changing focus of feminist concern. She finds intolerable a society where blueprints for female enslavement and "gynocide" abound. A study of actual female enslavement that goes beyond specific practices to examine the larger political, social, and economic issues involved.

Bode, Janet. *Fighting Back.* New York: Macmillan Co., 1978.

Although primarily about rape and organizing to stop it, the chapter called "A Common Goal" describes efforts to end all forms of "physical and psychological violence against women." Several antipornography efforts and organizations are described.

Brophy, Julia, and Carol Smart, eds. *Women In Law: Explorations in Law, Family, and Sexuality.* Boston: Routledge & Kegan Paul, 1985.

This collection of new essays explores the ways in which legal ideology and practice affect women and looks at issues such as child custody, domestic violence, and prostitution in the light of new research. The contributors review the history of feminist involvement with the law and analyze the law's fundamental failure to improve the status of women. They also assess strategies for change in view of the current backlash against women's rights and the traditional role of law in the subjugation of women. Although only marginally related to the specific topic of this bibliography, the book is included because it expresses a foundation of beliefs for those who wish to use law and legislation to meet the concern of women in a "campaign on pornography and violence against women. . . ."

Brownmiller, Susan. *Against Our Will: Men, Women and Rape.* New York: Simon & Schuster, 1975.

The chapter "Women Fight Back" is said to have opened the debate between feminists and liberals on what should be done about pornography. Brownmiller deals with the issues of verbal freedom, the 1970 report of the President's Commission on Obscenity and Pornography, sexual freedom, and the conservative and the liberal positions. She believes that the women's perspective demands a new approach. Brownmiller calls pornography "the undiluted essence of anti-female propaganda." She suggests that liberals, who are so quick to recognize propaganda used against other groups, should apply those same insights to women.

Burstyn, Varda, ed. *Women Against Censorship.* Vancouver, B.C.: Douglas and McIntyre, 1985.

A collection of essays by feminists opposed to attempts to ban pornography. Practical strategies for dealing with pornography without resorting to censorship are presented. Contributors fear that any attempts to ban materials could be turned against women's writing in the future. Included are the following: "Political Precedents and Moral Crusades: Women, Sex, and the State" by Varda Burstyn; "Second Thoughts" by Myrna Kostash; "Pornography: Image and Reality" by Sara Diamond; "A Capital Idea: Gendering in the Mass Media" by Lisa Steele; "Censorship and Law Reform: Will Changing the Laws Mean a Change for the Better?" by Lynn King; "Women and Images: Toward a Feminist Analysis of Censorship" by Anna Gronau; Mariana Valverde and Lorna Weir's "Thrills, Chills, and the 'Lesbian Threat' or, The Media, the State and Women's Sexuality." Other essays are Ann Snitow's "Retrenchment versus Transformation: The Politics of the Antipornography Movement"; June Callwood's "Feminist Debates and Civil Liberties"; "False Promises: Feminist Antipornography Legislation in the U.S." by Lisa Duggan, Nan Hunter, and Carole S. Vance; and "Beyond Despair: Positive Strategies" by Varda Burstyn. Appendix I is "Making Sense of the Research on Pornography." Appendix II presents "Excerpts from the Minneapolis Ordinance."

Byerly, Greg, and Rick Rubin. *Pornography: The Conflict Over Sexually Explicit Materials in the United States, An Annotated Bibliography.* New York: Garland Publishing, 1980.

This book is a selective, annotated bibliography on pornography encompassing psychological, sociological, religious, philosophical, legal, and popular perspectives. Emphasis is on works published in the 1970s, and it is useful for works beyond the scope of this book because it covers scientific studies and the whole field of study, opinion, and writing.

Califia, Pat. "A Personal View of the History of the Lesbian S/M Community and Movement in San Francisco." In *Coming to Power,* edited by SAMOIS. Boston: Alyson Publications, 1982.

A history of events surrounding the emergence of the lesbian sadomasochistic community of San Francisco. Califia says, "The women's movement of the sixties and early seventies was a hostile environment for sadomasochistic women." She says: "By 1978, the feminist antipornography movement was very powerful in San

Francisco. Women Against Violence in Pornography and the Media had hundreds of members . . . and they frequently attacked S/M and S/M imagery in their literature." She details "a long conflict with WAVPM. . . ." When WAVPM hosted "Feminist Perspectives on Pornography," the first national conference of the antiporn movement, SAMOIS was told it wasn't invited.

Califia, Pat, Lisa Duggan, Kat Ellis, Nan Hunter, et al. *Caught Looking: Feminism, Pornography & Censorship*. New York: Caught Looking, 1986.
   A collection of writings from members of the Feminist Anti-Censorship Task Force. Gathered into this one volume are previously published works by Pat Califia, "Among Us, Against Us: The New Puritanism"; Ellen Willis, "Feminism, Moralism and Pornography"; Paula Webster, "Pornography and Pleasure"; Nan Hunter, Carole Vance, and Lisa Duggan, "False Promises"; and Kate Ellis, "Why I'm Black and Blue from the Rolling Stones and Don't Know How I Feel About It." In addition to these reprints there is a new piece, "Sex Premises," by Barbara O'Dair and Abelyn Tallman. The book contains a chronology, a bibliography, and many illustrations of "100 Years of Porn." There is also an annotated text of the MacKinnon-Dworkin ordinance proposal for Minneapolis.

Carter, Angela. *The Sadeian Woman and the Ideology of Pornography*. New York: Pantheon Books, 1978.
   Carter presents a definition of the Marquis de Sade, of pornography and patriarchy, and examines whether or not he believed unrestrained sexual practices were as liberating for women as for men.
   The *New Republic*, 1 September 1979, 31–33, contains a review of this book by Robin Morgan.

Delacoste, Frederique, and Felice Newman, eds. *Fight Back: A Resource Book on Feminist Resistance to Male Violence*. Minneapolis: Celis Press, 1981.
   Many contributions document violence toward women and the organizing of women to resist that violence. Included are reports of actions taken against pornographers. Nikki Craft describes "The Incredible Case of the Stack O'Prints Mutilations," at the University

of California. The Preying Mantis Womens' Brigade also reports on some of its activities against pornographers.

Diamond, Irene. "Pornography and Repression: A
Reconsideration." In *The Criminal Justice System and Women*,
edited by Barbara Raffel Price and Natalie J. Sokoloff. New
York: Clark Boardman Co., 1982.
A discussion of pornography in a general consideration of victimization of women is relevant because, as Diamond says, "the real subject of pornography is not sex, but power and violence." Diamond argues that the pornographic depiction of women as victims reinforces and fosters attitudes of domination of women. Further, Diamond claims, this leads to actual physical brutalization and victimization. Diamond reviews findings from a national commission on violence attitude surveys, retrospective studies of convicted sex offenders who reported on their experiences with pornography prior to their committing crimes, laboratory studies, and social indicator studies. Diamond summarizes all types of available research and rejects the Commission on Obscenity and Pornography findings that pornography is harmless.

Donnerstein, Edward. "Pornography and Violence Against
Women: Experimental Studies." *Annals of the New York
Academy of Sciences*, 1980.
Brief reports on research to examine the effects of certain media presentations on aggression against women. "The present research suggests that specific types of media" may account for violence against women. The chapter includes extensive references to research reports.

Donovan, Josephine. "Women's Studies Scholarship: The Voice of
the Mother." In *The Women's Annual 1984–1985*, edited by
Barbara Haber. Boston: G.K. Hall & Co., 1985.
There is only a brief mention of women and pornography in this essay surveying issues in feminist theory. It is included for background information on feminist theory—the liberationists versus the radical feminists—and the information that those who find sadomasochism, pornography, and "other fringe sexual practices" defensible are "liberation feminists." Mary Daly questions here

whether the views presented at the 1982 Feminist IX conference held at Barnard are feminist at all.

Dworkin, Andrea. *Our Blood: Prophecies and Discourses On Sexual Politics*. New York: Harper & Row, 1976.
A collection of addresses delivered by Dworkin between 1974 and 1976. In "The Root Cause" she discusses the role pornography plays in reinforcing female negation. "In literary pornography, the pulsating heart of darkness at the center of the male-positive system is exposed in all of its terrifying nakedness."

Dworkin, Andrea. *Pornography: Men Possessing Women*. New York: Perigree, 1981.
Theoretical discussion of the link between pornography and men's oppression of women. Chapters on "Power," "Men and Boys," "the Marquis de Sade," "Objects," "Force," "Pornography," and "Whores." There is an extensive bibliography at the end of this book. Dworkin records the root meaning of *pornography:* "it means writing about whores . . . contemporary pornography strictly and literally conforms to the word's root meaning."

Dworkin, Andrea. *Right-Wing Women*. New York: Perigee, 1983.
Discussion of the radical right's notions of what women are for, what meaning is assigned to women's lives, and how women fight for meaning, often by attaching themselves to men and to their values. Many references are listed in the index to pornography and perceptions of it by the "Right."

Dworkin, Andrea. *Women Hating*. New York: E.P. Dutton, 1974.
This book is, in the words of the author, "an action, a political action where revolution is the goal." It is part of an effort to restructure the community to end male dominance. The author describes and analyzes the treatment of women throughout history. Pornography is part of this treatment of women.

Eysenck, Hans J., and D.K.B. Nias. *Sex, Violence and the Media*. New York: St. Martin's Press, 1978.
This book, included because of frequent references to it in other cited publications, is concerned with the possible influence that

viewing and reading violent pornography may have on a person's behavior. The authors say that many believe that increasing violence and sex in the media may be responsible for undesirable changes in our civilization. Others believe pornography and violence may make possible "the birth of a new society." Both sides "accept without question that the media in fact have an effect on the behavior, the outlook and the mental climate of viewers and readers." This study examines the evidence to support or refute the view that the media do influence people. Two statements made by the authors are: "There is ample evidence that media violence increases viewer aggression," and "That pornography has effects on viewers and readers can no longer be disputed, but their effects can be quite variable."

Faust, Beatrice. *Women, Sex and Pornography: A Controversial Study.* New York: Macmillan Co., 1980.
The author considers the differences in sexuality and sexual response in men and in women and how this affects their attitude toward pornography. She cites the theory that gang rape is meant not to debase women but "to show off to other males" and that rape in wartime is a way of "coping." Faust chronicals a lack of interest in pornography by women and says "we need to admit that differences between males and females exist and that they derive from an interaction of culture with biology." She doubts the connection made between pornography and violence against women. She attempts to chart the interrelation of pornography, the sexual revolution, and the women's movement. She examines the reactions of feminists as well as the content of the pornographic material.

Garry, Ann. "Pornography and Respect for Women." In *Philosophy and Women,* edited by Sharon Bishop and Marjorie Weinzerg. Belmont, Calif.: Wadsworth, 1979.
This book is intended for the general reader who wants to "systematically rethink the meaning of sex roles." Many topics are covered. Ann Garry's chapter refers back to one by Robert Baker called "Sex and Language" where he states that words for sexual intercourse show that women are not seen as full human beings, "and instead the act involves harm done to the woman." Garry uses the results of Baker's study to suggest that the connotation of sex as involving harm to women is responsible for the fact that pornogra-

phy is seen by women as degrading. She says it will be necessary to break the connection between sex and harm "in order to have nonsexist, nondegrading pornography."

Griffin, Susan. *Made From This Earth; An Anthology of Writings.* New York: Harper & Row, 1982.

The author argues, in the chapter called "Pornography and Silence," that "pornography is an expression not of human erotic feeling and desire, and not of a love of the life of the body, but of a fear of bodily knowledge, and a desire to silence eros." She says that the pornographer has historically been treated as a brave crusader for human liberation but that this liberation is not necessarily meant to include women.

In another chapter entitled "Sadism & Catharsis: The Treatment Is the Disease," the argument that without pornography there would be more rape and violence against women is refuted, even though men are quoted as seeing themselves as brutal and uncontrollable. There is detailed discussion of this argument and why it appears fake to the author.

Griffin, Susan. *Pornography and Silence: Culture's Revenge Against Nature.* New York: Harper & Row, 1981.

For the author, pornography is a crucial expression of modern culture and a contradiction of the best natural instincts. She describes the contents of pornographic books, films, and magazines. She analyzes the tragic effects, both social and psychological, on the polarization of men and women. Griffin says: "Men are torn asunder by repressive cultures that oppose soul to body and will to instinct as the dualism of good and evil; men renounce the sensual and deny their physical affinity with nature for fear of losing control and relapsing into the weakness of feeling. Since they despise what they long for—the tender sensitivity of the vulnerable self—they mutilate it in vengeful fantasies."

Marcia Yudkin said, in a *Ms* magazine review (*Ms* 40, January 1982, 41): "*Pornography and Silence* is profound, stimulating, sophisticated, far-reaching in its implications. Although feminists are still left wondering about the First Amendment and a conscionable strategy to make pornography disappear, we are much enriched. . . ."

Groult, Benoite. "Night Porters." In *New French Feminisms: An Anthology*, edited by Elaine Marks and Isabelle de Courtivron. Amherst: University of Massachusetts Press, 1980.

Groult declares pornography just the same old male image of woman-hate, particularly virulent at this time because women have become different and "are overthrowing the glorious tradition of feminine humiliation which has been the basis for masculine pride, the things that are setting off a hysterical, sadistic rage in all those who cannot accept giving up the fascinating and degrading relationship between hangman and victim." Her essays details the treatment of women in classical and avant-garde French literature. Of the latter she says it is nothing new, nothing revolutionary. "This is very old language which even occasionally admirable style cannot justify." She says we must be wary of the rehabilitation of de Sade and that it is only his imprisonment and censorship that put him on a pedestal when, in fact, he is very boring to read. Groult sees the case of de Sade as a good argument against censorship. She regrets that "erotic-pornographic books—at least those written by man—have the serious drawback of being sad."

Kappeler, Susanne. *The Pornography of Representation*. Minneapolis: University of Minnesota Press, 1986.

The author develops the point that the content of pornography is largely irrelevant; patriarchal power resides in the structure of representation itself. She theorizes that all representation, as Western culture has come to understand it, is in some sense pornographic because it makes an object of the person or thing presented. It is possible for men to be made into objects but not often in our culture. Kappeler says men look at women the way people look at animals, and provides evidence for this opinion. She believes "the fundamental problem at the root of men's behavior in the world toward women is the way men *see* women." She is opposed to the establishment of any official group formed to police pornography.

Kittay, Eva Feder. "Pornography and the Erotics of Domination." In *Beyond Domination: New Perspectives on Women and Philosophy*, edited by Carol C. Gould. Totowa, N.J.: Rowman and Allenheld, 1984.

The aim of this essay is to explore the moral-political questions concerning the objectionable nature of pornography in its causal aspect as hate literature and as hate literature with a sexual charge. Second, it aims to consider pornography's aspect as a symptom of certain social and political relations between men and women, asking "what we can learn about sexual relations in a sexist society by looking at the limiting case of pornography." The author gives examples of what she and other feminists call pornography. Kittay, in discussing the definition of pornography, says the crucial distinction is not between erotic art and pornography but between what is erotic and what is pornographic. Other subjects considered are legitimate versus illegitimate sexuality, sadomasochistic sexuality, pornography and misogyny, pornography as hate literature, and the harm of pornography considered as hate literature. Kittay concludes this essay by saying: "The problem, in the end, is more than pornography. It is the eroticizing of the relation of power. The eroticism of domination, rather than being demanded by the nature of eros, is an instrument for the maintenance of male perogatives."

Klein, Freada. "Violence Against Women." In *The Women's Annual 1982–1983,* edited by Barbara Haber. Boston: G.K. Hall & Co., 1983.

A survey of the various forms violence against women takes and how small are the resources devoted to coping with them. Klein says there has been little research lately on pornography and violence against women. She is very critical of Susan Gray's analysis of existing research (cited in this bibliography) "which seems to accept violence against women as a given, not to be changed." Instances of resistence to pornography by women are noted. Extensive references follow the chapter.

Kostash, Myrna. "Whose Body? Whose Self?: Beyond Pornography." In *Still Ain't Satisfied: Canadian Feminism Today,* edited by Maureen Fitzgerald, Connie Guberman, and Margie Wolfe. Toronto: Women's Educational Press, 1982.

Raises the issue of pornography and freedom of speech from a Canadian, feminist perspective. Considers the violence of pornography and its effect as hate literature against women. Kotash's article points out: "It is often difficult to know who are our allies in our attempts to combat misogyny. There is the dilemma of trusting state censorship when it is a state that seldom acts in the interests of women. And we reject an alliance with prudery." This article weighs the issues of sexual and intellectual freedom on the one hand with the outrages against women on the other. Canadian organizations and actions are noted and a short list of references included.

Kuhn, Annette. *The Power of the Image: Essays on Representation and Sexuality.* Boston: Routledge & Kegan Paul, 1985.
   The author states that "From its beginnings, feminism has regarded ideas, language, and images as critical in shaping women's (and men's) lives." In this book Kuhn addresses the various issues regarding the representation of women, including feminist ideas and concerns. Chapters include "Living Dolls and 'Real Women'," "Lawless Seeing," and "Sexual Disguise and Cinema," among others. In the index there are numerous references to pornography. In the chapter "Lawless Seeing" Kuhn discusses pornography and why this subject is difficult for the feminist writer.

Lederer, Laura, ed. *Take Back the Night: Women on Pornography.* New York: William Morrow & Co., 1980.
   A collection of over thirty essays providing a feminist critique of pornography. It is dedicated to "the thousands of women who recognize the hatefulness and harmfulness of pornography, and who are organizing to stop it now." Sections included are: "What is Pornography?," "Who is Hurt?," "Who Benefits?," "Research on the Effects of Pornography," "Pornography and the First Amendment," "Taking Action and Looking Ahead." There are references and a bibliography. Among the contributors to this collection are Kathleen Barry, Pauline Bart, Judith Bat-Ada, Megan Boler, Charlotte Bunch, Phyllis Chesler, Irene Diamond, Andrea Dworkin, Martha Geve, Marge Piercy, Florence Rush, Alice Walker, and many others. Some of the contributions are unique to this book; others reprinted from other sources.

Lorde, Audre. *Sister Outsider.* Trumansburg, N.Y.: The Crossing Press, 1984.
   In the chapter "Uses of the Erotic: The Erotic as Power," Lorde describes the erotic resource within each woman and how it has been suppressed by male oppression. She says the erotic is often confused with pornography. "But pornography is a direct denial of the power of the erotic, for it represents the suppression of true feelings." Lorde says women empowered are seen as dangerous.

Lynn, Barry W. *Polluting the Censorship Debate*. Washington, D.C.: American Civil Liberties Union, 1986.

Lynn, who attended all the Meese Commission hearings and testified before it, has written the ACLU rebuttal to the commission's *Final Report*. "Tragically," he writes, "the Commission's final recommendations endorse virtually nothing which could make a real difference to the genuine victims of a still sexist culture." (Annotation prepared from secondary source.)

McNall, Scott G. "Pornography: The Structure of Domination and the Mode of Reproduction." *Current Perspectives in Social Theory* 4, 1983, 181–203.

It is argued that pornography is central to the subordination of women in modern society, as part of the process whereby people come to internalize modes of domination and subordination. It is shown that pornography is part of the ideological sphere, a means whereby the social relations of production are reproduced, and a part of the patriarchal ideological system, though expressed in varied ways. The symbol system of a society is related to the maintenance of the social structure, which often means that it supports male dominance. To illustrate these ideas, the symbol systems of the Mbum Kpau of Africa, the Mundurucú of Brazil, and the Dani of New Guinea are examined; all have rituals or beliefs that legitimate, normalize, and mystify male dominance. So it is with modern pornography, which portrays women as incompetent, irrational, animalistic, at the mercy of their hormones, easy, available, and alienated. A political strategy is suggested to educate people to the meaning of pornography.

Malamuth, Neil, and Edward Donnerstein. "The Effects of Aggressive-Pornographic Mass Media Stimuli." *Advances in Experimental Social Psychology* 15, 1982, 103–136.

This report of a research project is included in this bibliography because Malamuth and Donnerstein are often cited by feminists in the antipornography movement. The authors state that although the U.S. Commission on Obscenity and Pornography (1970) found "no evidence that pornography had antisocial effects," some investigators are critical of the commission's conclusions. The purpose of this chapter in this annual publication is "to address one aspect of the issue that was not adequately addressed by the commission's research: the effects of stimuli that combine sexuality and aggression."

The Meese Commission Exposed. New York: National Coalition
    Against Censorship, 1986.
    This is the proceedings of a public information briefing on the U.S. Attorney General's Commission on Pornography, sponsored by the National Coalition Against Censorship in New York City on 16 January 1986. Leanne Katz, executive director of NCAC, explains the purpose of the meeting in her opening remarks, "This briefing is to impart some sense of the broad range of views which are being ignored while important social policy is under consideration. The remarks of the people we invited should make us all stop and think—and worry—and then act, to fight censorship." The fourteen speakers include Colleen Dewhurst, president of Actors' Equity Association, Kurt Vonnegut, Barry Lynn of ACLU, Lisa Duggan for FACT, Eve Paul of Planned Parenthood, and Betty Friedan, among others.

Millett, Kate. *Sexual Politics.* Garden City, N.Y.: Doubleday, 1970.
    The author describes the relationship between the sexes as political, a continuing power struggle. She shows how the patriarchal bias operates in culture and is reflected in literature. There are references to pornography in the text. Millet says the easy access to pornography has made male hostility more obvious in recent times.

Morgan, Robin. *The Anatomy of Freedom.* Garden City, N.Y.:
    Anchor Press, 1982.
    Morgan says, in the chapter "The Stake in the Heart: An Anatomy of Sexual Passion," that she believes sexual violence is the "cultural synonym for sexual energy." One of the forces perpetuating this distortion is pornography. She discusses the recent research linking pornography and sexual violence, and "The New Pornocracy"—the porn aristocracy. In this discussion, she charges Ellen Willis, Pat Califia, and three others of being pro-pornography and pro-sadomasochism. "And surely such women can realize that what they, in their piteously twisted sexuality, are upholding has nothing to do with the feminist vision of freedom."
    For Willis's response to this attack see the *Village Voice Literary*

Supplement, December 1982, 16–17 listed in the "Newspaper" section.

Morgan, Robin. *Going Too Far: The Personal Chronicle of a Feminist.* New York: Random House, 1977.

In the chapter "Theory and Practice: Pornography and Rape," Morgan discusses the myths and fictions of rape—calls it an act of political terrorism. She argues against outright censorship but describes different strategies aimed at hurting the business of pornography and making the customers embarrassed. Notes that the massive porn industry grinds on and lists the possible effects on women. Morgan says "Pornography is the theory, rape is the practice," an analogy often quoted in the antipornography movement.

Nobile, Philip and Eric Nadler. *United States of America vs. Sex.* New York: Minotaur Press, Ltd., 1986.

The authors, who describe themselves as "journalists of sexual politics," attended the Meese Commission hearings around the country. Their book chronicles the commission's hearings and "the lack of its intellectual rigor." When commissioner Ellen Levine asked when they were going to discuss what they would consider pornographic, the commission chair, Henry Hudson replied, "I appreciate your bringing it up, but I don't know [if] that's within our province." Testimony of witnesses before the commission is included, from elderly Mary in Chicago who suffered from sexual abuse during the French-postcard era of porn to Catharine MacKinnon and Nan Hunter (also in Chicago) and Andrea Dworkin in New York City. The book includes the Becker-Levine dissenting report. The author's have also compiled a report of a "Shadow Commission." They asked eleven other citizens to comment on the commission's report. "Unlike the government investigators, this body abhors censorship and is willing to consider erotica dispassionately and without bias." Statements from Betty Friedan and Marcia Pally are among the eleven.

Poggi, Dominique. "A Defense of the Master-Slave Relationship." In *New French Feminisms: An Anthology.* Amherst: University of Massachusetts Press, 1980.

Poggi says pornography is a defense of the master-slave relationship that controls the sex act. "In point of fact, the sex act, as it appears in porn films, is a rape . . . always presented after the act 'as utterly fulfilling.' " Poggi sees actual rape as a threat to keep women in line, dependent on a male, and pornography as a propaganda tool to reinforce this same end. Whereas the feminist movements are demanding that women be allowed to control their own bodies, pornography proposes women's bodies be at the disposal of all men. The film *Emmanuelle* is cited as a case in point.

Robson, Ruthann. "Pornography, Power, and the First Amendment." In *Alternative Library Literature 1982–1983: A Biennial Anthology,* edited by Sanford Berman and James Danky. Phoenix: Oryx Press, 1984.
The author discusses the dilemma of being both a feminist and a lawyer during the current conflict over pornography and the First Amendment. She notes that when the subject comes up her "bearded liberal associates immediately shout 'First Amendment' as if they were holding up a cross to Dracula." She notes that the First Amendment is "not without exceptions," and discusses problems of defining pornography, censorship, obscenity, and the First Amendment. Robson says: "Pornography attempts to silence female speech. . . . But women (and men) who believe that pornography is just as much a cancer in society as censorship must refuse to be silenced . . . must exercise our First Amendment rights to protest and to end the pornographic images of women and children."

Russ, Joanna. *Magic Mommas, Trembling Sisters, Puritans and Perverts: Feminist Essays.* Trumansburg, N.Y.: The Crossing Press, 1985.
Collection of feminist essays on questions of sexuality and pornography. Gives careful attention to analysis of women in a patriarchy, and the need to develop a theory to deal with a male–dominated society. Some chapter headings are "Being Against Pornography," "Pornography by Women for Women, With Love," and "Pornography and the Doubleness of Sex for Women."
See also the review of this book by Marilyn Frye in *The Women's Review of Books,* August 1985 and another, lengthy review in *Off Our Backs,* December 1985.

Scott, David Alexander. *Pornography—Its Effects on the Family, Community, and Culture.* Washington, D.C.: The Child and Family Protection Institute, 1985.

Scott believes that the goal of the pornography industry is "validating, legitimizing, and promoting deviance and addiction." He worries that this is detrimental to the stability of marriage and the family. He says that among the prominent opponents of pornography are feminist groups and that they "narrow their definition of pornography to sexual acts in conjunction with violence against women." He goes on to say that "Some feminist groups do not object to very graphic sexual depictions. A small number of radical lesbian splinter groups are even largely uncritical of homosexual pornography. . . ." There are chapters on "Pornography Effects," "Contents of Pornography," "Television Violence Research," and "The Role of Organized Crime," among others. The publication concludes with the statement, "The joy and contributions of chaste and mature love are incompatible with pornography and its effects." There are copious footnotes.

Smith, Margaret, and Barbara Waisberg. *Pornography: A Feminist Survey.* Toronto: Boudicca Books, 1986.

This pamphlet is a bibliography of feminist perspectives on pornography. The list covers fifty American, Canadian, and British books and articles from a variety of perspectives. There are four sections: sexuality, social construction of perception, perspectives on pornography, and control of pornography. Every entry is described.

Smith, Margaret, and Barbara Waisberg. *The Pornography Workshop for Women.* Toronto: Berch Associates, 1984.

This is a workbook to be used by anyone wishing to plan a workshop for women around the issues of pornography. It is a very detailed how to guide covering such topics as "Hopes and Fears Exercise," "Erotica and Pornography: Definitions and Distinctions," "Guide for Analyzing Pornography," "Examination of Pornographic Material," "The Pornography Industry," and "Values and Messages in Pornography." Resources to be used are included and methodology described. There is a bibliography of mostly Canadian material.

Snitow, Ann, Christine Stansell, and Sharon Thompson. *Powers of Desire: The Politics of Sexuality.* New York: Monthly Review Press, 1983.

In the introduction the authors point out that "sex is, unquestionably, a public topic and a highly political one" but that the talk has all been done by men until recently. "Feminism has cast its new, if variable, illumination on the subject of sex." The introduction traces the history of sexual politics, including the antipornography movement which emerged in the late 1970s. The feminist, anti-pornography movement is examined critically and countervailing feminist attitudes toward pornography are presented. Of particular relevance to this bibliography are the essays by Ann Snitow on "Mass Market Romance: Pornography for Women Is Different"; by Carole S. Vance on "Gender Systems, Ideology, and Sex Research"; by Alice Echols, "The New Feminism of Yin and Yang"; and "Feminism, Moralism and Pornography" by Ellen Willis. The bibliographic notes following each chapter are extensive.

Sobel, Alan. *Pornography: Marxism, Feminism, And The Future of Sexuality.* New Haven: Yale University Press, 1986.

The author presents a Marxist perspective on pornography. He defends pornography's "valuable aspects" and examines the relationship of the means of production to male sexual power and reasons that in an ideal communist society the content and distribution of pornography would be different and not degrading to women. He also analyzes the feminist position and criticizes it from his political viewpoint. (Annotation prepared from a secondary source.)

Steinem, Gloria. *Outrageous Acts and Everyday Rebellions.* New York: Holt, Rinehart & Winston, 1983.

In the chapter "Erotica vs. Pornography" there is discussion on the confusion over pornography, obscenity, erotica, and the entanglement of sex and violence. Steinem says there is very little erotica—women have seldom been free enough to pursue such pleasures. She finds the First Amendment argument against feminist antipornography, "the most respectable and public opposition, but also the one with the least basis in fact."

"Testimony Against Pornography: Witness from Denmark." In
*Crimes Against Women: The Proceedings of the International
Tribunal,* edited by Diana Russell and Nicole Van de Ven.
Millbrae, Calif.: Les Femmes Publishing, 1976.

There are frequent references in this work to Denmark which
got rid of censorship laws and claims that sex crimes are down as a
consequence. In this interview, a young Danish woman speaks
against this view and the "legalization of women as sex objects." This
book ends with "Proposals Relating to Particular Crimes" and on
page 195 of this chapter there is a recommendation from the
international workshop on pornography.

Tong, Rosemarie. *Women, Sex and the Law.* Totowa, N.J.: Rowman
and Allanheld, 1984.

In the introduction the author states the reason for the writing
of this book, "Although feminist scholars have written many excel-
lent books and articles on pornography, prostitution, sexual harassment, rape, and woman-battering, there have been few systematic
efforts to analyze the legal theories and practices that bring these
diverse issues under the same scrutiny." In addition to this she
addresses crucial differences in perspectives—men, women, lesbians,
heterosexuals, blacks, whites—to ask why different kinds of women
have suffered in different sorts of ways at the hands of Anglo-
American law for the same reason—their sexuality.

U.S. Attorney General's Commission on Pornography. *Attorney
General's Commission on Pornography: Final Report.*
Washington, D.C.: U.S. Dept. of Justice, 1986.

This two-volume, 1,960 page report contains the conclusions
of the commission's year-long inquiry into the impact of pornography on American society. The report begins with biographies of the
commission members (in which the marital status of the women is
given, but not of the men), followed by individual statements. These
statements generally reflect the areas where the commission was not
in agreement. Commissioners Becker and Levine wrote, "Consequently, while we endorse many of these recommendations, we
dissent on some, for reasons of critical policy differences, lack of

clarity and more importantly, because evidence essential to a considered evaluation of the proposals was not presented."

The chapter on "Laws and Their Enforcement" quotes from the MacKinnon-Dworkin ordinance. Noting the courts have found it unconstitutional, the commission goes on to state: "First, we are in substantial agreement with the motivations behind the ordinance, and with the goals it represents." In the chapter on "Civil Rights" the commission's recommendation eighty-seven is "legislatures should conduct hearings and consider legislation recognizing a civil remedy for harm attributable to pornography." In support of this recommendation the report states: "The civil rights approach, although controversial, is the only legal tool suggested to the commission which is specifically designed to provide direct relief to the victims of the injuries so exhaustively documented in our hearings throughout the country." Later in the report, in the chapter on "Victimization," the testimony of Andrea Dworkin is quoted at length.

Vance, Carole S., ed. *Pleasure and Danger: Exploring Female Sexuality*. Boston: Routledge & Kegan Paul, 1984.

Papers gathered from the Scholar and the Feminist IX Conference held at Barnard College in 1982. Covers many diverse topics such as the myth of the perfect body, the sexual socialization of children, the ideology of popular sex literature, and more. The epilogue written by Carole Vance provides her view of the controversy that developed during and after the conference. Many references to the antipornography movement and the organization, Women Against Pornography, can be found in the index. The view that those who are opposed to pornography are against sex is alluded to in some arguments. There is a long review of this book by Cindy Patton in *Womens Review of Books,* December 1984 and in the September 1985 issue of *Sojourner.*

Vidal, Gore. "Women's Liberation Meets the Miller–Mailer–Manson Man." In *Homage to Daniel Sharp: Collected Essays, 1952–1972.* New York: Random House, 1972.

The essay, originally published in *The New York Review of Books,* 22 July 1971, documents the hatred of certain representative men for women. "Men do hate women and dream of torture, murder, flight." He has a paragraph on pornography. He says it is no accident that in the United States the phrase "sex and violence is used as one word. . . ."

Wagner, Sally Roesch. "Pornography and the Sexual Revolution: The Backlash of Sadomasochism." In *Against Sadomasochism: A Radical Feminist Analysis*, edited by Robin Ruth Linden, et al. Palo Alto, Calif.: Frog in the Well, 1982.

The premise of this essay is "we learn our sexual behavior and we learn it from the culture in which we live." The article examines our collective experience and how it accounts for present sexuality. Pornography is described as "the propaganda which indoctrinates men into the sexual power they have over women and teaches men how to manifest that power." A distinction is made between the sexual revolution "which we have had, and actual sexual liberation." Much of the article is devoted to the emergence of lesbian sadomasochism and how this mirrors the dominant male culture. Several pages of notes follow the article. Other essays in the collection are at least tangentially relevant to the topic of feminists and pornography.

Williamson, Jane, Diane Winston, and Wanda Wooten, eds. "Pornography." In *Women's Action Almanac*. New York: William Morrow & Co., 1979.

A survey of feminist attention to the changes in pornographic images, especially the violent degradation of women. There is a brief report on the first national conference, "Feminist Perspectives on Pornography," November 1978 in San Francisco. Examples of media abuse of women are given. The First Amendment consideration is also noted as is the economics of the pornography industry.

Willis, Ellen. *Beginning to See the Light*. New York: Knopf, 1981.

One essay, "Feminism, Moralism, and Pornography," written in 1979, was one of the earliest feminist critiques of the growing antipornography movement. The author lists the arguments used by the feminists in the antipornography movement and why she believes "they miss the point, confuse issues and detract from the overall context of women's oppression." Willis says, "I find myself more and more disturbed by the tenor of antipornography actions and the sort of consciousness they promote; increasingly their focus has shifted from rational feminist criticism of specific targets to generalized, demagogic moral outrage."

Wilson, Carolyn F. *Violence Against Women: An Annotated Bibliography.* Boston: G.K. Hall & Co., 1981.
This 100 page bibliography plus index is a guide to hundreds of journal articles and books on many aspects of violence against women. Chapters include "Battered Women," "Rape," "Sexual Abuse of Children," and "Pornography." In the chapter on pornography there is a section headed "Feminist Response."

Zellman, Dolf. *Connection Between Sex and Aggression.* Hillsdale, N.J.: Lawrence Erlbaum Associates, 1984.
This book, outside the defined limits of this bibliography, is noted here to assist the reader because it has been cited often in other books and articles included in this bibliography. In the words of the author, this book seeks to cover "the pertinent theoretical and research developments in all disciplines that have significantly contributed to our understanding of interdependencies between sexual and aggressive behaviors."

2.
Magazine Articles

The articles referred to in this section cover the period from 1970 to 1985, with a few references for 1986. The publications are many and various. Included are scholarly journals, such as the *Journal of Personality and Social Psychology* and the *Harvard Women's Law Review*, and popular magazines like *Esquire*, *Vogue*, and *Psychology Today*. Others are aimed at specific interest audiences—feminist and/or lesbian, for instance. Although articles from law journals are included, articles on law cases or First Amendment issues are not unless they bear directly upon the feminist controversy over pornography. The same can be said for most research studies on the effects of pornography on behavior. A few are listed because of their frequent citation in many of the publications included. Annotations in this section, as in all sections, quote the material itself and do not reflect the points of view of the authors of this bibliography.

"ALA's Intellectual Freedom Committee Responds to Pornography Commission Report." *American Libraries*, September 1986, 580–581.
  The committee met at ALA headquarters in August of 1986 to prepare an advisory statement on the U.S. Attorney General's Commission on Pornography. The statement is printed here. It points out conflict with the First Amendment, the flawed methodology of the commission's work, the absence of significant debate at the hearing. The ALA statement calls for all those who support the First Amendment to work together since "much that the commission advocates is not consistent with that Amendment or even with current obscenity laws."

Allen, Gina. "What Those Women Want in Pornography."
  Humanist 38, November–December 1978, 46–47.
  The author describes antipornography feminists as against violence and the degradation of the female and not as being antisex. She says she is "always disappointed that they don't include in their protests the granddaddy of all Western pornography—the Bible. It is in the Bible—and in the patriarchal culture that produced it and

continues to hold it sacred—that women are first dehumanized. . . ."
She believes that by changing the values of our society and culture
we will change the nature of pornography from the violent to the
erotic.

Alter, Ann Ilan. "Pornography and Feminism: Divisive Relations
    Explored." *New Directions for Women*. January–February 1985,
    12.

Alter gives a brief survey of the history of pornography and
attempts, since the eighteenth century, to suppress it. She notes the
Comstock Law of 1873 "designed to protect the public from
obscene literature, denied women basic medical information about
contraception and gynecology." She believes this could easily happen
again. "Feminists have everything to lose in such a situation, for
once the fight against pornography is won, abortion, birth control,
and day care will not be far behind. These too are obscenities to
those who believe that women's place is in the home."

Anderson, Alison. "Cleaning Up the Cosmos: Women Write About
    Pornography." *Hecate* 8, 1982, 97–101.

A brief analysis of the attention to pornography in the feminist
movement and what that attention tells about the movement itself.
Susan Griffin's *Pornography and Silence*, Andrea Dworkin's *Pornography*, and Beatrice Faust's *Women, Sex and Pornography* are examined.
Anderson believes Griffin and Dworkin paint themselves into a
corner where "every aspect of culture is porn, so porn is the central
issue, so women must call for its censorship." Faust, on the other
hand, "is as interested in feminist reactions to pornography as in the
content of the material itself. Her scope allows for a lucid presentation of what data do exist on the social meaning and uses of porn,
the variance in its effect on men and women, and whether this
variance has any significance to the position of women." The books
by Dworkin, Faust, and Griffin are included in this bibliography.

"Andrea Dworkin Fights." *New Directions for Women*,
    November–December 1985, 1.

Report of a $150 million libel suit filed by Dworkin against
Larry Flynt and *Hustler* magazine. Central to the suit are cartoons
and pictures of women engaged in sexual acts, which are labeled as
Andrea Dworkin. NOW is represented in the suit because of claims

that the treatment of Dworkin causes other women to be afraid to fight pornography.

Armstrong, Louise. "Diversity on Diversion?" *The Women's Review of Books* 3, October 1985, 1, 4–5.
In a long essay, reviewing a book on the contemporary feminist movement (*Controversy and Coalition: The New Feminist Movement,* by Myra Marx Ferree and Beth B. Hess. Boston: Twayne Publishers, 1985) the author recounts current conflicts related to the antipornography movement and the strain this has caused her when thinking about feminism. She notes the censorship of a Women Against Pornography slide show by the Women and Law Conference, the letters against FACT and its *amicus* brief—filed against the pornography and civil rights ordinance authored by feminists.

Ashley, Barbara Penchkowsky, and David Ashley. "Sex as Violence: The Body Against Intimacy." *International Journal of Women's Studies* 7, September–October 1984, 352–371.
"This paper discusses the feminist critique of pornography and reviews contemporary hard-core pornography in the light of this critique." It is argued that human sexuality must be interpreted and understood as meaningfully scripted behavior. The dramatic growth in hard-core over the last decade has necessitated the standardization of particular pornographic themes that both express and mask domination and violence. This denial of domination and violence is facilitated by a sexual scripting which presents a highly reified version of human sexuality and which portrays highly artificial and individualized forms of sexuality as strongly naturalistic.

Atwood, Margaret. "Atwood on Pornography." *Chatelaine,* September 1983, 61, 118, 126, 128.
A brief summary of antipornography activities in Canada followed by Margaret Atwood's definition of pornography. She poses some questions about how society is to deal with it. Atwood says "It is naive to think of violent pornography as harmless entertainment. . . . We should find out exactly what its effect is and then make some informal decisions about how to deal with it." Atwood describes some personal experiences which illustrate the "two poles of emotionally heated debate that is now thundering around this issue." She believes the central question to ask in the debate over violent

pornography is "What's the harm?" She believes that harm may not have been proven but neither has the "no-harm" position. Atwood believes society must find out in a hurry.

Bachy, Victor. "Danish 'Permissiveness' Revisited." *Journal of Communications* 26, Winter 1976, 40–43.

A personal account of some statistics and impressions of the consequences of lifting the ban on pornography—five years later. Says there is no proof that crime rates were affected one way or another, and that "we certainly cannot conclude that it has improved." He goes on to describe a working-class neighborhood destroyed by porn shops.

Baldwin, Margaret. "The Sexuality of Inequality: The Minneapolis Pornography Ordinance." *Law and Inequality: A Journal of Theory and Practice* 2, 1984, 629–653.

This article describes the Minneapolis ordinance which "seeks to redress injuries demonstrably suffered by women as a class through the production and consumption of pornography." The author summarizes the facts and legal theory underlying the city council findings and the "relief afforded by the ordinance." Extensive footnotes and references follow this article.

Barkey, Jeanne. "Minneapolis Porn Ordinance." *Off Our Backs* November–December 1985, 1.

Cover article on the Minneapolis City Council's consideration of amending its civil rights ordinance to include pornography as an act of sex discrimination. This article lists the elements found in the ordinance which define pornography for the purpose of this statute. A history of antipornography activity in Minneapolis is written too along with a brief summary of argument "for" and "against."

Bart, Pauline, Linda Freeman and Peter Kimball. "The Different Worlds of Women and Men: Attitudes Toward Pornography and Responses to 'Not a Love Story' A Film About Pornography." *Women's Studies International Forum* 8, 1985, 307–322.

Men and women viewing the antipornography film were surveyed about their attitudes toward it. Women were much more negative toward pornography than the men, and their beliefs and attitudes were changed more by the film. Many other factors about differing responses are reported by the researchers. The authors conclude that gender-free, humanist standards "according to which pornography could be evaluated do not exist, and that approaches to pornography control based on its role in the particular oppression of women are valid."

Baumgarten, Laurie. "Thoughts on Pornography." *Union W.A.G.E.*, January–February 1979, 9–10.

Baumgarten attended the Feminist Perspective on Pornography conference held in San Francisco, 17–19 November 1978. This essay is a result of all the information she gained there. First she believes the Women's Alliance to Gain Equality should include a clear position on this issue as part of its purpose and goals. Secondly she feels: "Our task is to convert an anger that is immobilizing in its intensity into an anger that is determination to bring about change. We must attack sexism wherever it occurs. But we must also remember that we live in the era of monopoly capitalism and it is the profit-system which is the economic base of these attacks on women."

Bearchell, Chris. "No Apologies." *The Body Politic*, February 1986, 26–29.

Article on how the strippers and other sex workers feel about feminist actions and attitudes toward pornography. The author says that "as the legal and political assault on them escalates, feminist sex workers are defining their own issues for a change." One woman interviewed at "Challenging Our Images," a conference on pornography and prostitution, is quoted as saying, "I'm tired of these people who think they can condemn our business without even talking to the women who work in it."

Beckworth, Barbara. "Women and Pornography Symposium." *Sojourner: The Women's Forum*, November 1985, 13–15.

Report of a symposium in October where feminists debated "pornography as a social policy issue" and the antipornography ordinance on which Cambridge, Massachusetts residents were to vote in November. Catharine MacKinnon, Carole Vance, Norma Ramos, Leland Pierce, and Evaline Kane were some of the speakers.

The text of the antipornography ordinance is printed. The article is followed, on pages 14–15, by "Readers Speak Out on the Porn Ordinance."

In this same issue of *Sojourner* there are, on the "letters" page, references to the antipornography movement in response to a review of Carole S. Vance's *Pleasure and Danger* which had appeared in the September 1985 issue. Vance's book is included here in the "Books" section.

Berger, Alan. "The Porn Wars Heat Up: Is Censorship an Option?" *The Real Paper*, 14 July 1979, 14.

Berger presents an overview of antipornography activities, from a trashing of a Harvard Square bookstore and other direct actions by Marcia Womongold to various speakers on the subject of pornography as violence against women. Writer Tillie Olsen is quoted as saying that "the sudden, overwhelming explosion of pornography in the past few years coincided with the social changes wrought by the women's movement," and that the coincidence could hardly be fortuitous. Pornography, she suggested, "is the ideological element of a counter-revolution against women." Berger describes the split between feminists and civil libertarians. "Defining pornography as death threats against a female population in rebellion . . . feminists are less and less willing to share with civil libertarians the very terms of discourse that have been traditionally used to debate the question of censorship and free speech." Berger suggests that: "civil libertarians—and all the rest of us—should start looking around for ways to protect women from the violence endemic to a violent society. . . . If we can't do anything about that kind of criminal conduct, then sooner or later we're going to have to try cauterizing one of the causes with censorship."

Berry, John. "Drawing the Line." *Library Journal* 104, 15 November 1979, 2385.

Berry's editorial describes the actions of feminists against pornography and says, "We librarians will undoubtedly be asked again to choose sides between the 'knee-jerk' purism of the American Library Association's intellectual freedom establishment 'and the anti-pornography activists.' " He says that most Americans have had little trouble "drawing the line" regarding censorship on the one hand and freedom of expression on the other, that in fact there are a number of exceptions to protection of expression by the First Amendment. He has no trouble "drawing the line" when it comes to "that new, violent porn purveyed in Times Square." He hopes other librarians will draw that same line.

Bessmer, Sue. "Anti–Obscenity: A Comparison of the Legal and the Feminist Perspectives." *Western Political Quarterly* 34, March 1981, 143–155.

A brief description of the history of support for censoring obscene or pornographic materials. Then this essay attempts to define what is obscene or pornographic from a feminist point of view and how this definition compares with other formulations of the concept of obscenity employed by other groups. Finally, the author examines possible "theoretical justifications for the suppression, by some means, of that which is deemed objectionable."

Blachford, Gregg. "Looking at Pornography," *Screen Education,* Winter 1978–1979, 21–28.

The author says that "pornography, as a 'cultural' product of society can be examined to find the connection between its images and industry and the wider society's dominant values, attitudes and assumptions." He attempts a definition of pornography, the business and the images, and the present political struggle over its legal status.

Blachford, Gregg. "Looking at Pornography: Erotica and the Socialist Morality." *Radical America,* January–February 1979, 7–18.

Author says that one contribution of feminists to socialist political practice is its stress on applying political theory to private life—the idea that the "personal is political." He then attempts to analyze pornography from a socialist perspective and "what our attitudes as gay male socialists should be."

Blakely, Mary Kay. "Is One Woman's Sexuality Another Woman's Pornography." *Ms,* April 1985, 37–47, 120–123.

Views of the antipornography activists and their opponents; a chronology of actions in the movement arena; and notes on groups, articles, and proposed legislation. The author points out that many

former allies in social actions and issues now find themselves opposing each other and that they "disagree vehemently over how to deal
with pornography." The text of a model antipornography ordinance
as proposed by MacKinnon and Dworkin is included. The July 1985
issue of *Ms* prints several pages of letters in response to this article.

Bonavoglia, Angela. "America, Apple Pie and Pornography: Do
   Feminists Stand a Chance?" *USA Today,* May 1981, 28–31.
   Reports on how pornography has become "an institution in the
U.S. today that is fast becoming as American as apple pie." The
author says there is evidence of its legitimacy everywhere and
presents examples. There is chronological step-by-step notice of how
the feminists became involved with the issues including demonstrations against the film *Snuff,* and pressured Warner Communications
to tear down its billboard advertising a Rolling Stones album. In
1978 Women Against Violence in Pornography and Media held the
first feminist conference on pornography in San Francisco. However, the group that must be credited with catapulting pornography
as a feminist issue onto the national stage is New York City's Women
Against Pornography (WAP), founded by Susan Brownmiller in
1979. There are descriptions of the early Times Square actions and
details on the contents of WAP's slide show. The arguments of those
who believe pornography is violence against women are given as are
those of the "porn-as-liberated fun" tradition.

Bonavoglia, Angela. "Tempers Flare Over Sexuality Conference."
   New Directions For Women, July–August 1982, 15.
   A report on the Barnard College Women's Center conference,
Towards a Politics of Sexuality. Describes the picketing of the
conference by Women Against Pornography and the literature they
distributed criticizing the conference. Bonavoglia regrets that the
conference did not include a broader spectrum of women. "An
attempt to integrate the feminist movement's commitment to protecting women from sexual danger with a commitment to freeing
women for sexual experimentation and expression is understandable
and perhaps overdue, but must we disown one another to do it?"
   The September–October issue carries a letter from Women
Against Pornography complimenting Bonavoglia's article for accuracy and insight, but also pointing out that it skirted "a central point:

the ideas promoted by the conference organizers were in direct opposition to the principles of feminism."

Bosmajian, Haig A. "Obscenity, Sexism and Freedom of Speech." *College English* 39, March 1978, 812–814, 819.

Bosmajian says that the sexism in obscenity laws lies in the fact that restricting materials because they may lead to antisocial behavior in men, also deprives women of those materials. "Yet we have the Nixon [Supreme Court] appointees saying, in effect, that the mature female population . . . can be deprived of seeing or reading 'obscene' materials because there is a possibility that such materials might tend to incite some of the sixty-three million adult males 'to violent or depraved or immoral acts.' "

Brod, Harry. "Eros Thanatized: Pornography and Male Sexuality." *Humanities in Society* 7, Winter–Spring 1984, 47–63.

A critical interpretation of the ways in which many of pornography's images of sexuality alienate and repress men as well as women. It is argued that pornographic images have restricted male sensuality. An attempt is made to bridge the perspectives of the women's and men's movements, and to assess the motivations and potentialities for a men's antipornography movement, using concepts derived from Sigmund Freud, G. W. F. Hegel, and Karl Marx. Arguments used to enlist men in crusading against pornography have usually been based solely on moral appeals, asking them to give up the satisfaction they receive from pornography for essentially altruistic reasons. Such appeals assume that men do receive real pleasure from pornography, and that a stance against it requires them to give up on moral grounds an inherently desirable aspect of male privilege. It is argued here that in being asked to give up pornography men are being asked to give up disadvantages, not advantages.

Brooke. "Feminist Conference: Porn Again." *Off Our Backs,* November 1979, 24–27.

A report of the then six-and-a-half month-old Manhattan-based group, Women Against Pornography, which put on a conference to discuss pornography as a feminist issue. The conference attracted 700 to 800 women. There is detailed information on the organization itself, its work, and its philosophy. There were films, slide show, a speak-out. There were workshops, including one on "Women in the Pornography Business," and on many other topics including violence and pornography. The controversies at this conference are reported on as well.

Brooke. "Life, Liberty and the Pursuit of Porn." *Off Our Backs*, January 1979.

Report of an all-day colloquium at the New York University School of Law, 2 December 1978, on "Violent Pornography: Degradation of Women versus Right of Free Speech." The speeches are reported under the symposium title elsewhere in this bibliography. This gives some additional views of the speeches and proceedings from an observer.

Burt, Mary. "Use of Pornography by Women: A Critical Review of the Literature." *Case Western Reserve Journal of Sociology* 8, September 1976, 1–16.

The apparent lack of interest of women in pornography can be explained better by sociological rather than by biological factors. Sex-role and socialization concepts can provide a major part of such an explanation. The assumption of many studies that inherent physiological differences account for women's lack of interest is not tenable, given these other considerations. The literature on this subject is critically reviewed, and suggestions are made for new approaches to research.

Califia, Pat. "See No Evil—The Anti-Porn Movement." *The Advocate*, 3 September 1985, 35–39.

Califia provides a view of the historical development of efforts to pass legislation, designed by Dworkin and MacKinnon, which would define pornography as sex discrimination and outlaw it as a violation of women's civil rights. She dissects the language of the legislation to see if in fact, as the supporters say, its effects would be limited to "violent pornography." She analyzes and compares the usual meaning of the term pornography and its definition in the proposed bill. Her view of activities and personalities in Minneapolis, then Indianapolis and Suffolk County, New York are reported. Califia says that even though the bill has failed everywhere, "We should worry because this model porn bill creates moral panics wherever it goes. In its wake it becomes easier to pass more traditional obscenity laws." The Meese Commission on Pornography, its membership and its activities are described. Califia closes her article by noting that there is more than one opinion among feminists about the "anti-porn crusade." This article is one of the few that makes any attempt to look at connections between the anti-pornography ordinance struggle and the Meese Commission on Pornography by setting each in the continuum of historical activity around the issues of pornography and sexuality.

Callahan, Jean. "Women and Pornography: Combat in the Video Zone." *American Film*, March 1982, 62.

Author says films on cable television are bringing pornography out of sleazy downtown theaters and into the privacy of the home, "where women, who have traditionally been only its subjects, are fast becoming a new audience for it." The author goes on to say that all women are not happy about that prospect, and she wonders if there is a relationship between pornography and violence, and if so, "might not cableporn swell those statistics of wife beating and rape within marriage?" There follows a description of various antipornography activities and the critics of these activities. Comments on some of the new films are included too.

"Cambridge Anti-Porn Initiative Loses." *Off Our Backs*, January 1986, 18.

Reports rejection of the Cambridge antipornography ordinance, sponsored by the Women's Alliance Against Pornography, based upon the model statutes drafted by Catharine MacKinnon and Andrea Dworkin. A summary of the positions of the various area women's organizations is included.

Carlan, Andrew. "Feminists Join Anti-Porn Crusade." *Conservative Digest*, November 1982, 38.

Notes that feminist anger at smut peddlers may result in a new alliance of feminists and the New Right. Lists "zap" awards given by Women Against Pornography for examples of sexist advertising. The author says, "Feminists are beginning to think that they may have inadvertently set themselves up for what they now see as humiliating. . . ."

Carlin, David R., Jr. "Hegel and Pornography: The Limits of
Personel Taste." *Commonweal,* 1 November 1985, 599–600.

A discussion of the "split currently opening up in the feminist
community in the United States over the explosive issue of women,
pornography and the law." More details on the arguments on
various sides in the debate. The author says "feminists can't have it
both ways . . . either there is a sphere of absolute privacy—and then
my tastes in pornography, no matter how demeaning to women, are
nobody's business but my own; or there is no such sphere—and then
the law, in an attempt to protect the dignity and good name of one
half the human race, has, at least in principle, the right to interfere
with trade in pornography."

Carpenter, Ted Galen. "Porn Busters." *Reason,* October 1985,
26–30.

Carpenter says, "It was a most curious spectacle in April 1984 as
members of the Indianapolis City Council debated an anti-pornography ordinance." He describes an unlikely coalition of left-wing
feminists and conservative Republicans. Arrayed against them was
an alliance of booksellers, theater owners, and the American Civil
Liberties Union. A history of the fate of the ordinance follows.
Carpenter points out that it makes pornography actionable under
civil law, rather than the usual criminal offense of material found
obscene. He details what he believes would be the negative actions
and results if such an ordinance finally became law. Carpenter
concludes his article by saying: "it doesn't matter whether censorship
assumes the guise of orthodox obscenity statutes or the newer and
more insidious mask of bogus civil-rights measures. The ultimate
consequences are identical—less freedom, more tyranny."

Charbonneau, Claudette. "Sexual Confusion at Barnard." *Off Our
Backs,* June 1982, 25, 29.

In a commentary and analysis of the Barnard conference,
Charbonneau is very critical of it and its exclusion of ideas or
perspectives contrary to those of the organizers. She notes her shock
at hearing, at a feminist conference, the antipornography movement
"being ridiculed for attacking *male* values." She reports that some of
the organizers insisted that "there was no need to present the
feminist case against pornography because their views are well
known."

"Charges of Exclusion and McCarthyism at Barnard Conference."
Off Our Backs, June 1982, 5, 19–21.
One of the most controversial aspects of the Barnard conference
was a leaflet called, "We Protest," from a Coalition for a Feminist
Sexuality and Against Sadomasochism, composed of Women
Against Pornography (New York), Women Against Violence
Against Women (Los Angeles), and New York Radical Feminists.
The issues surrounding the leaflet include its accuracy, its analysis,
the exclusion of certain viewpoints from the conference, charges of
McCarthyite tactics, freedom of expression, and the right to criticize.
Those who supported the leaflet, and those who did not had intense
feelings about it. Reactions and name-calling are reported here in
some detail. Pornography plays a role in each side of the controversy.

Chervenak, Mary Francesca. "Selected Bibliography On
Pornography and Violence." *University of Pittsburgh Law
Review* 40, 1978, 652–660.
List of scientific studies on pornography and violence. The
author states that "we believe this bibliography represents the best
current opinion and research on pornography and its effects."

Cheuvront, Beverly. "New York Bill to Loose 'All Hell on Earth.' "
New Directions for Women, January–February 1985, 13–14.
Article discussing the possibility of introducing a bill in New
York City similar to the Minneapolis antipornography ordinance.
The "clash between opponents and proponents will be 'all hell on
earth,' according to Andrea Dworkin." A major change in the New
York bill is a "provision that isolated passages won't be construed to
be pornographic," Dworkin said. The ACLU and FACT are both
quoted as being strongly against such a bill. Ann Snitow, of FACT,
said, " 'It's a false hope that if we could get rid of pornography, we
could get rid of male violence.' "

Chute, Susan. "Backroom With the Feminist Heroes: Conference
for Women Against Pornography." *Sinister Wisdom* 15, Fall
1980, 2–4.
Chute's impression of the 1979 "Conference for Women
Against Pornography" in New York City. Recitation of some of the
testimony of speakers and of women in the audience and a report of

confrontation between some lesbian feminists and "straight" feminists.

"Citizens for Media Responsibility Without Law." *Off Our Backs,*
    May 1986, 6.
    Account of two protests against pornography organized by
Citizens for Media Responsibility Without Law. One demonstration
was at a B. Dalton bookstore for selling *Penthouse.* The second
protest was at the Playboy Building. One protester said: " 'Besides
exploiting children, the Playboy empire is built on the bodies of
women.' "

Claire, Roxanne. "Women and Pornography." *Isis International
    Bulletin* 18, 1981, 24–25.
    Summary of the issues in the antipornography movement. The
author says laws against pornography would be useless because they
are administered by male lawyers and judges. "We should note that
while the First Amendment ultimately protected James Joyce and
Henry Miller in their exercise of 'freedom of speech' the same cannot
be said for Margaret Sanger in her attempt to distribute birth control
information."

Colker, Ruth. "Legislative Remedies for Unauthorized Sexual
    Portrayals: A Proposal." *New England Law Review,* 20,
    1984–1985, 687–720.
    "Unauthorized sexual portrayals of models and actresses are
alluring and commercially profitable. Yet these portrayals can harm
the professional reputation and emotional well-being of the individuals portrayed. Although these individuals frequently bring invasion
of privacy actions to redress their injuries" these actions usually fail
because judges label the individuals involved public figures and
therefore excluded from laws against invasions of privacy. The
author, in this article proposes a "legislative remedy for unauthorized
sexual portrayals that would provide new protection for all plaintiffs
and particularly for many models and actresses." The proposed
statute provides all individuals with the right to consent "unless the
portrayal has the primary purpose of being to impart news." Existing
legislation is examined, laws and actions are surveyed, and, in Part
III, it is argued "that the proposed legislation would survive consti-

tutional challenge on the ground that protection from sex-based violations of civil rights can justify restrictions on free speech." There is considerable discussion of the work of Catharine MacKinnon and Andrea Dworkin and many detailed citations to articles on feminists and pornography.

Colker, Ruth. "Moving Toward Common Ground on the
    Pornography Issue." *Off Our Backs,* June 1985, 10–11.
    Analysis and commentary on the MacKinnon-Hunter debate at the Sixteenth National Women and the Law Conference. The author, a lawyer, points out the unanswered questions and the unresolved issues. She emphasizes that there are shared concerns and proposes alternatives to the current attempts to resolve the controversy resulting from different feminist perspectives relating to pornography.

Colker, Ruth. "Pornography and Privacy: Towards the
    Development of a Group-Based Theory for Sex-Based
    Intrusions of Privacy." *Law and Inequality: A Journal of Theory
    and Practice* 1, 1983, 191, 201–205.
    "This article explores privacy doctrine to show the pervasive ways that male norms of sexuality enter and control women's lives. Feminists may understand that the personal is political; law remains adverse to such an understanding. In particular, feminists often unthinkingly value privacy, not recognizing that the current legal conception of privacy helps maintain women's oppression. This article challenges that unquestioned assumption." The author also discusses the arguments made by radical feminists in the antipornography movement. "The radical feminist critique of pornography, however, does not allow such an easy accommodation; radical feminists use pornography and all examples of women's sexual abuse as an opportunity to critique the norms of sexuality themselves. Because the pervasive use of women as sex objects is consistent with the norms of sexuality, courts refuse to recognize women's abuse. Male jurisprudence defines the problem of female sexual abuse narrowly and is indifferent to women's oppression. Hence, it maintains the objectifying norms of sexuality."

"Coming Apart: Feminists and the Conflict Over Pornography."
Off Our Backs, June 1985, 6–8.
Excerpts from the Sixteenth National Women and the Law
Conference workshop entitled "Pornography: A Feminist Response." The two debaters are Catharine MacKinnon, antipornography activist and coauthor of the Indianapolis antipornography
ordinance, and Nan Hunter of FACT. The report of the debate is
followed by extensive commentary from others including speakers
from the audience, the *Off Our Backs* collective, FACT, and FAP
(Feminists Against Pornography, a Washington, D.C. organization).

Cottingham, Laura. "Pornography—Expression or Oppression?"
WIN, 15 July 1982, 10–14.
A survey of the antipornography issue within the feminist
movement, noting the debate has shifted from being between male
liberals and feminists to a debate between feminists. The writer
rejects the anti-antipornography feminists' argument that "antipornography equals anti-sex." She believes, "Unless we say no, we
are continuing to be the best possible slaves to misogynist culture."

Court, John H. "Pornography and Sex Crimes: A Re-Evaluation in
Light of Recent Trends Around the World." *International
Journal of Criminology and Penology* 5, 1976, 129–157.
A collection of evidence from several countries on the relationship between the availability of pornography and sex crimes. The
author concludes from the evidence collected that "the stable trends
reported here invalidate the claim that the sex-crime problem will be
reduced by making pornography freely available, and give extensive
support to the hypothesis that serious sex-crimes are on the increase."

"A Court Test for Porn." *Newsweek,* 13 August 1984, 40.
News report on the Indianapolis ordinance which would "allow
local residents who feel their rights have been violated by pornographic materials to file a complaint with the city's Office of Equal
Opportunity." Report reviews the various opponents and proponents of the ordinance which was, at the time, being reviewed by
Federal District Judge Sarah Evans Barker.

D'Amico, Robert. "The Meaning of Pornography." *Humanities in Society* 7, Winter–Spring 1984, 87–101.

"Consideration of three models for the study of the connection between sexuality and violence in pornographic literature or images: the feminist power theory (so called because sexuality is treated as a secondary effect of certain power relations), sociobiology, and Sigmund Freud. Contrary to expectations, especially in view of feminist criticisms, these three theories reach a significant consensus with only minor differences. Pornography is an exclusively male phenomenon, emotionally linked to agression, instinctually rejected by women, and concealing a puritanical moralism." It is concluded that the main issue in attacks on pornography such as those of Andrea Dworkin (*Pornography: Men Possessing Women*, New York: Perigee Books, 1979) and Susan Griffin (*Pornography and Silence*, New York: Harper & Row, 1981) is a moralism concerning images and representation. Each of the books named above are entries in the "Books" section.

"David Cohen Represents NYLA Before Meese Commission on Pornography," *NYLA Bulletin* 34, February 1986, 4, 6.

Report on the testimony of David Cohen, New York Library Association's Intellectual Freedom and Due Process Committee member, before the Attorney General's Commission on Pornography at the New York City hearing on 22 January 1986. Cohen "stressed the role of the library in a democratic society as the one place striving to provide people with open access to needed information without intimidation and moral prejudice. . . ." Cohen completed his testimony by pointing out that the "commission should be most concerned about the constant stream of attempts to remove materials from libraries or to censor them so as to be unavailable to specific segments of our society."

De Crow, Karen. "Strange Bedfellows." *Penthouse*, May 1985, 96–97.

De Crow, a lawyer and former NOW president, equates being against pornography with being against sex. She criticizes the attempts to pass laws to regulate pornography.

D'Emilio, John. "Women Against Pornography." *Christopher Street* 4, 1980, 19–26.

Describes his trips to Times Square as a young male homosexual and then later to support women protesting a pornographic film called *Snuff*. More recently he went to the area to see the slide show and take the tour organized by Women Against Pornography. He says he went because he was confused about the issues of violence and pornography and because he found himself condemning WAP from secondary sources and wanted to find out more for himself. He is very critical of the slide show, the tour and the interpretations WAP applies to some materials. He says, "During the discussion I became convinced that Women Against Pornography is at best misguided and at worst downright dangerous." He believes they are antisex not against violence.

Dershowitz, Alan M. "Partners Against Porn." *Harpers,* May 1985, 22.

This is from an essay that appeared as part of a symposium in the December 1984 issue of *Film Commentary* (see entry here under "Pornography: Love or Death?"). Dershowitz says antipornography feminists have "made their Faustean pact with the devil—the Reverend Jerry Falwell and his gang of fundamentalist censors." He continues with his arguments against censorship for any of the reasons given by the feminists.

Diamond, Irene. "Pornography and Repression: A Reconsideration of 'Who' and 'What.' " *Signs: Journal of Women in Culture and Society* 5, Summer 1980, 686–701.

Diamond takes a critical look at some of the studies and research experiments which shaped the Report of the Commission on Obscenity and Pornography (1970) and examines the assumptions upon which they were built.

For a more detailed annotation see under "Diamond, Irene" in the "Books" section.

Diamond, Irene, and Lee Quimby. "American Feminism in the Age of the Body." *Signs: Journal of Women in Culture and Society* 10, Autumn 1984, 119–125.

The authors see problems in the use of the language of control by feminists to discuss sexuality. They stress the need for a contextual approach that does not define identity as equivalent to sexuality or separate sexuality from its historical context. They question the beliefs that sexuality is in fact central to identity, an "ultimate truth," and basic to liberation.

Donnerstein, Edward. "Aggressive Erotica and Violence Against Women." *Journal of Personality and Social Psychology* 39, 1980, 269–277.

This article, outside the limits established for this bibliography, is included here because the work of Donnerstein is cited so often.

"To examine the effects of aggressive-erotic stimuli on male aggression toward females, 120 male subjects were angered or treated in a neutral manner by a male or female confederate. Subjects were then shown either a neutral, erotic, or aggressive-erotic film and given an opportunity to aggress against the male or female via the delivery of electric shock. Results indicated that the aggressive-erotic film was effective in increasing aggression overall, and it produced the highest increase in aggression against the female. Even nonangered subjects showed an increase in aggression toward the female after viewing the aggressive-erotic film. Results are discussed in terms of the arousal and aggressive cue value of the films."

Donnerstein, Edward, and Daniel Linz. "Mass Media Sexual Violence and Male Viewers." *American Behavioral Scientist* 29, May–June 1986, 601–618.

This essay examines research on violent pornography and summarizes work to date. Topics included are "Aggressive Pornography and Sexual Arousal," "Aggressive Pornography and Attitudes Toward Rape," "Aggressive Pornography and Aggression Against Women." There is another section with the heading "The Influence of Nonpornographic Depiction of Violence Against Women." The authors conclude "this research strongly suggests a potential harmful effect, from exposure to certain forms of aggressive pornography and other forms of sexualized violence." There are three pages of references.

Donovan, Mary Ellen. "Feminists and Porn." *The Nation* 232, 3–10 January 1981, 2, 20.

Donovan objects to the thesis of Aryeh Neier, cited in this bibliography, ("Memoirs of a Woman's Displeasure," *Nation,* 16–23

August 1980) that feminists have called attention to *Ordeal* (Lovelace, Linda and Mike McGrady, *Ordeal,* New York: Berkley Publishers, 1980) because Lovelace's story of victimization and coercion fits their ideology. She says Neier presumes that most feminists believe women appear in pornography only if forced to do so, but he does not substantiate this claim. She says Neier's knowledge of both feminist thought and the pornography industry are quite limited and gives her evidence for this statement. At the end of her critique, Mr. Neier is allowed a reply.

Douglas, Carol Anne. "Pornography: Liberation or Oppression?"
    Off Our Backs, May 1983, 14–15.
    The Fourteenth National Conference: Women and the Law in Washington, D.C. included a workshop on pornography which provoked heated debates and revealed strong splits among conference participants. Washington area Feminists Against Pornography presented a slide show. Ann Snitow, as part of a panel, suggested that antipornography activism had become important because it was easier to attack images rather than institutions. Pauline Bart, a sociologist on the panel, said research had led her to support the movement. Then Margo St. James, organizer of COYOTE, said she agreed with much of what Snitow said. St. James called pornography creepy and boring. "But prostitutes won't work against pornography until feminists work for decriminalization of prostitution. Ridicule is the most effective weapon against pornography," she said. Catharine MacKinnon spoke on her views regarding the relationship of law, pornography, and politics, reported here in some detail. Pauline Bart, as a challenge to Ann Snitow's views, recited a verse of hers, "Breathes there a woman with a mind complex who hasn't been called anti-sex?" Many questions and comments are reported from the audience. The author of this article notes her opinion that MacKinnon's speech drew the most applause.

Douglas, Carol Anne. "Towards a Politics of Sexuality." *Off Our*
    Backs, June 1982, 2–3.
    Report on the general sessions of the Barnard Conference. Many questions were raised, and a number of people spoke out about the antipornography movement. Alice Echols attacked the movement as being equivalent to the antiabortion movement. Nu-

merous exchanges between Echols and others are reported, including criticism that people in the antipornography movement were excluded from formal presentations.

Drexler, Rosalyn. "Sexual Fantasies, Pornography, and Women."
   Mademoiselle, July 1973, 126.
   Describes pornography, the ways in which it appears to be used by men, and contrasts it with her perceptions of what women value as fantasy. Drexler calls current pornography films "sex as science fiction." She says, "A woman viewing these films finds that she is being raped by a commercial force so vulgar that the only way to eliminate the experience is to suffer amnesia."

D'Souza, Dinesh. "The New Feminist Revolt: This Time It's
   Against Feminism." *Policy Review,* Winter 1986, 45–52.
   D'Souza believes the leaders of the feminist movement are "suffering post-feminist depression." This is in part because of political set-backs like the defeat of the E.R.A. The divisions in the feminist movement are also a result of "the negative fallout of the women's movement." Feminist supporters of sexual liberation "believed that as constricting social norms were set aside, sex could be freer and less perverted and consequently the demand for pornography would evaporate." In fact, the pornography industry flourished and the issue now divides feminists. "Now Dworkin blames not just the porn triumvirate—Hugh Hefner, Al Goldstein, and Larry Flynt—but the values of liberalism, feminism, and the sexual revolution itself for the social abuse that women suffer." D'Souza also discusses the "fall-out" from such issues as no-fault divorce, comparable worth, abortion and the feminization of poverty.

Duggan, Lisa, Nan Hunter, and Carol S. Vance. "False Promises:
   New Antipornography Legislation in the U.S." *SIECUS
   Report* 13, May 1985, 1–5.
   In the introduction to this article a SIECUS writer says that many organization members have been called upon to testify either on behalf of or against various new forms of antipornography legislation, and "A decision should not be made until the law's terminology and the full implication of its enactment is studied." In the introduction writer's view, Duggan, Hunter, and Vance have

done just that. The article itself describes the new laws and their "central flaw." The clauses in the ordinances are analyzed, one by one, and potential dangers for women in their application are noted.

Dworkin, Andrea. "Against the Male Flood: Censorship, Pornography, and Equality." *Trivia: A Journal of Ideas,* Summer 1985, 11–32.

Discourse on censorship, obscenity, pornography and pornographers, the subordination of women, and equality for women. Clear closing remarks on what civil rights law used against pornographers is intended to do. The "Model Anti-Pornography Law" is included. (Reprinted from the *Harvard Women's Law Journal* 8, 1985).

Dworkin, Andrea. "Against the Male Flood: Censorship, Pornography, and Equality." *Harvard Women's Law Journal* 8, 1985, 1–29.

For annotation, see above.

Dworkin, Andrea. "An Interview, With Louise Armstrong." *The Women's Review of Books,* 3 May 1986, 5–7.

Questions, answers, and discussion about Dworkin's writings, her political work, her involvement with the women's movement. Andrea Dworkin's recent novel *Fire and Ice* (London: Secker and Warburg, 1986) was published in England, because she could not find an American publisher who would accept it. Armstrong questions whether or not Dworkin's politics resulted in the novel being turned down. Dworkin believes it was definitely an act of censorship, provoked in part by her involvement with the antipornography movement. Dworkin provides other information on her views about pornography.

Dworkin, Andrea. "The Lesbian in Pornography: A Tribute to Male Power." *Sinister Wisdom* 15, Fall 1980, 73–74.

Details of pornography that supposedly portrays lesbian lovemaking but, in fact, barely resembles it. "The symbolic reality instead is expressed in the posture of women exposed purposefully to excite a male viewer." Dworkin analyzes the differences in the images and the reality.

Dworkin, Andrea. "Pornography's 'Exquisite Volunteers.' " *Ms,*
 March 1981, 65–66, 94, 96.

The article starts with the description of a woman in a *Playboy*
feature, from the German edition. The woman is called "an exquisite
volunteer." The author goes on to chronicle brutality against women
and relates this woman to the Jewish women exterminated by the
Germans. She describes also the victimization of women by male
scientists with their portrayals of the female—women resist force
because they wish to be conquered; they are masochistic; they like
pain. "She wants it; they all do."

Dworkin, Andrea. "Pornography: the New Terrorism." *The Body
 Politic,* August 1978, 11–12.

An article on the atrocities that have been directed at various
groups since the beginning of human history and how pornography,
with its frequent portrayal of women, fits into this history. Dworkin
says the oppressed are "encapsulated by the culture, laws and values
of the oppressor. Their behaviours are controlled by laws and
traditions based upon their presumed inferiority." Dworkin sees
pornography as an instrument of terror used against women as
propaganda to keep them in their place.

Dworkin, Andrea. "The Prophet of Perversion: A New Reading of
 the Marquis de Sade." *Mother Jones* 5, April 1980, 24–26,
 50–54.

Dworkin says Sade, the world's foremost pornographer, reigns
supreme. His presence is vivid in the proliferation of violent pornography. "Sade's most cherished values—the fusion of sex and violence—saturate the bulk of pornography currently produced." She
says those who fight the contempt for women that is the essence of
pornography fight Sade as he is embodied in "millions upon millions
of men. . . ." Dworkin describes Sade's life and the place in literature
and culture which others have accorded him.

Dworkin, Andrea. "Speech Exhorts March." *Off Our Backs,* January
 1979, 4–5.

This is a transcript of a speech Dworkin made before a march
against pornography in San Francisco. Dworkin starts her speech by

saying: "I searched for something to say here today quite different from what I am going to say. I wanted to come here militant, and proud and angry as hell. But more and more, I find that anger is a pale shadow next to the grief I feel. If a woman has any sense of her own intrinsic worth, seeing pornography in small bits and pieces can bring her to a useful rage. Studying pornography in quantity and depth, as I have been doing for more months than I care to remember, will turn that same woman into a mourner." The balance of the speech discusses pornography, what it is, what it does, and what it says about women.

This speech is also printed in *New Women's Times* 4, December 1978 and *Take Back the Night* under the title "Pornography and Grief." It is printed in *New Directions for Women,* November–December 1980, under the title "Pornography: A Hatred Without Bounds."

Eckhaus, Phyllis. "Pornography and Values." *Womanews* (New York City), September 1985, 14–15.

The author's position is that neither logic, nor law, nor social science will resolve the conflict between women who see pornography as dangerous to women and those who see the weakening of First Amendment rights as the greater danger. The issues in the dispute ultimately involve values.

Ehrenreich, Barbara, Elizabeth Hess, and Gloria Jacobs. "A Report on the Sex Crisis." *Ms,* March 1982, 61–62, 64, 87.

The authors note a present confusion over sexual permissiveness and sexual liberation. They report on some of the conflicts and confusions from a historical perspective. Authors note that the "first cracks in the feminist consensus appeared when women split over pornography." Gayle Rubin, Deirdre English, Charlotte Bunch, Andrea Dworkin, and Pat Califia are among those quoted.

Ellis, Kate. "I'm Black and Blue from the Rolling Stones and I'm Not Sure How I Feel About It: Pornography and the Feminist Imagination." *Socialist Review* 14, May–August 1984, 103–125.

Theories of female sexuality, the split that surfaced at the Barnard College conference in 1982, how the women's movement has viewed sex and power, the nature of women and of men—all of these are linked to the phenomena of the current antipornography movement.

Ellis, Kate. "Keeping the Enemy in Sight." *New Directions for Women,* May–June 1985, 10.

Ellis writes in response to an article by Leidholdt and Rush that appeared in the January–February 1985 issue of *New Directions for Women.* She recounts an assault she had suffered and concludes the muggers "were not under any illusion (derived from pornography or wherever else) that I enjoyed being treated like that." She believes there is a clear distinction between fantasy and real life and that the feminist antipornography efforts are wrong. "The Women's Movement can never totally purify the everyday world, but it can provide an environment that emphasizes the separation between fantasy and behavior that most people experience, rather than insisting that fantasy and behavior are an indivisible whole."

Ellis, Kate. "No Sexuality Without Representation: A Feminist View." *Changing Men,* no. 15, Fall 1985, 13.

Ellis describes violence to women, including herself. She says that fantasy is not necessarily dangerous and that "making something invisible is not the same as making it harmless." She reports that Donnerstein's tests, on students exposed to sex and violence, have results that do not support the antipornography movement.

Elshtain, Jean Bethke. "The New Porn Wars: The Indecent Choice Between Censorship and Civil Libertarianism." *The New Republic,*, 25 June 1984, 15–20.

A review of the antipornography ordinance's history in Minneapolis and Indianapolis and the "familiar dramatis personae: angry feminist antipornographers and equally alarmed civil libertarians. But in the background also lurk conservative and religious antipornographers on the one side, and pornographers themselves on the other. Troubled liberals and (some) radicals look on, unable to join either . . . camp." Elshtain then explains her views on how this situation came about and what modern pornograhy tells us about "the broader social landscape." She concludes with the suggestion that communities must put pornography in its place rather than seeking to eradicate it altogether.

Elshtain, Jean Bethke. "The Victim Syndrome: A Troubling Turn in Feminism." *The Progressive* 46, June 1982, 42–47.

Elshtain finds a growing tendency among women to see themselves as potential victims of crime "despite statistics to the contrary." She goes on to criticize antipornography feminists for capitalizing on this tendency, using language that "turns out to be the rhetorical equivalent of nuclear war." This, in turn, leads them to "maintaining a patronizing view of women's passivity." The proposed solutions to the problem of pornography put forth by the feminist movement "allies it with reactionary forces and sets up women as the *sole* arbiters of social morality and architects of social decency." Equally troubling is the feminists' celebration of freedom from sex role stereotypes, such as patriarchy, at the same time they demand "control over what individuals may see, hear, or read."

English, Deirdre. "The Politics of Porn: Can Feminists Walk the Line?" *Mother Jones* 5, April 1980, 20–23, 43–44, 48–50.

English writes about the reasons for her belief that attacks on pornography won't solve the problems of violence against women. She notes the link between feminist thought and behaviorism and how this has influenced the antipornography movement. Behaviorism suggests that sex-roles are learned, and that pornography teaches men to be violent toward women. Included is a description of Times Square porn shops and the activities of Women Against Pornography.

English, Deirdre, Amber Hollibaugh, and Gayle Rubin. "Talking Sex: A Conversation on Sexuality and Feminism." *Socialist Review* 11, July–August 1981, 43–62.

Discusses ideas of sexual freedom, changes in society, and the concern that some feminists have not accepted the new ideas and are as restrictive of individual variation as old psychiatric concepts. Other issues include the antipornography movement, violence against women, and the definition of pornography. The section headed "The Politics of Pornography" has interesting back-and-forth discussion about the writers' differing opinions on pornography. Gayle Rubin points out that NOW and the National Lawyers

Guild have taken stands against pornography, saying that it is violence against women. All want a critique of sexist pornography and a critique of antipornography movements.

"Evolution of a Feminist Art: Working at Wave." *Heresies: A Feminist Publication on Art and Politics* 2, issue 6, 1978, 86–88.

Women Against Violence Against Women "grew out of our realization that the way to eliminate the promotion of violence against women via the media was not through censorship, but through public education and consciousness-raising." The article reports on projects and strategies.

"Face Pornographer's Unequal First Amendment Rights, Women Work to be Heard; Seek Support for Their Rights." *Media Report to Women*, May–June 1985, 1, 7–16.

Most of this issue reports on feminist antipornography actions in several parts of the world. There is one page by editor Donna Allen entitled "Real First Amendment Question in Pornography Debate is Where are Our Rights?" She says the pornographer has all the rights. Judith Bat-Ada reports that there is an antiwoman blitz in Israel. Several news items note what is going on in other parts of the world including Canada and Great Britain.

Feator, Penelope. "Pornography." *Off Our Backs*, June 1982, 7.

Report of the Thirteenth National Conference on Women and the Law in Detroit and the workshop moderated by Patti Roberts, entitled "Pornography: the Free Spirit Debate." Other workshop leaders were Ann Manley of Ohio State Legal Services; Margo St. James of COYOTE; Priscilla Alexander from an antipornography group and Judith Walkowitz, professor at Rutgers University. Roberts objected to the title of the workshop saying that it focuses attention on legal discussion and away from pornography as woman-hating propaganda. She said most feminists in the movement don't want to put more power into the hands of the state. St. James wants to decriminalize prostitution and have more power over the production, use, and profit from pornography. Walkowitz compared the present antipornography movement to nineteenth century British feminist activities and questioned whether the current movement is a useful political strategy for feminists trying to empower and protect women. She details her objections to a variety of projects of women who are against pornography.

Ferguson, Ann. "Pleasure, Power, and the Porn Wars." *The Women's Review of Books*, 3 May 1986, 11–13.
An essay on the divisions in the feminist actions and discussions about pornography. Ferguson contrasts the views of those calling themselves pro-sex feminists with the views of most radical feminists and provides an in-depth philosophical and political analysis of the contrasting principles.

Ferguson, Ann. "Sex War: The Debate Between Radical and Libertarian Feminists." *Signs: Journal of Women in Culture and Society* 10, Autumn 1984, 106–112.
Ferguson contrasts the sexual attitudes of radical feminists who stress the primacy of intimacy and condemn many sexual practices as tied to male dominance, to the attitudes of libertarian feminists, who stress the primacy of pleasure and accept any sexual practices based upon mutual consent. The opinions of both groups appear to be based on oversimplified views of sexuality and on not properly recognizing the historically conditioned character of sexuality.

Feshbach, Seymour, and Neal Malamuth. "Sex and Aggression: Proving the Link." *Psychology Today*, November 1978, 111–122.
These two UCLA researchers say there is a link between sex and violence in our society. They note the growing amount of violence in sex magazines. They say, "At UCLA, laboratory research that we have been doing suggests that sexual arousal and aggression may be mutually enhancing in our culture . . . materials that are sexually explicit can stimulate aggressive behavior." They go on to describe their research and what it means to the control of pornography. (Included here because the work of these two researchers is often cited.)

Fields, Howard. "Women's Anti-Porn Law Looms in Senate." *Publisher's Weekly*, 12 October 1984, 13.
Describes possible antipornography actions being brought to Congress. Says proposed laws "would treat pornography as a viola-

tion of the civil rights of women and children." Notes groups supporting and groups speaking against this type of ordinance. Senator Arlen Specter of Pennsylvania, is quoted as believing such laws against pornography were "worthy of study and analysis."

Fithian, Nancy. "Take Back the Night." *Off Our Backs,* November
  1981, 9.
  A report of the Take Back the Night March on 26 September 1981 in Washington, D.C. The march was cosponsored by the Rape Crisis Center, D.C. Feminists Against Pornography, and others from the women's community. Approximately 900 people gathered and marched through the business and pornography districts. There is a description of the march, the area it traversed, and some responses to it.

Fleming, Thomas J. "Censorship: When to Say No." *Chronicles of
  Culture* 9, February 1985, 4–5, 35.
  Fleming reviews the current antipornography groups, finding "the new censorship coalitions are beginning to resemble a weekend at Fire Island," and the various arguments they support. He feels, however, that "rather than all this talk of rights, it would be refreshing to hear the censorship question expressed in the language of social obligation." He finds every society censors deviant behavior in the name of the common good. "This obligation cannot be expressed as a question of individual rights. It is a collective responsibility for the common good. In this respect, the feminists are as wrong as the pornographers."

"Forum: Playboy Sues Meese." *Playboy,* August 1986, 46.
  On 16 May 1986 Playboy Enterprises, the American Booksellers Association and others filed a lawsuit against U.S. Attorney General Meese; Alan Sears, the executive director of the Attorney General's Commission on Pornography; Henry E. Hudson, the chair of the commission; and each member of the commission. The suit, which is detailed in this report, was begun as a response to a letter written by Sears—on Justice Department letterhead—to corporations stating that they had been identified as being "involved in the sale of pornography." The purpose of the suit is "to stop this

blacklisting and any other actions that could curtail the free distribution of lawful and constitutionally protected publications."

Freedman, Estelle B., and Barrie Thorne. "Introduction to 'The Feminist Sexuality Debates.' " *Signs: Journal of Women in Culture and Society* 10, Autumn 1984, 102–105.

This records the stages of political awareness of women and sexuality. These authors state: "In the mid-1970s . . . feminist discussions of sexuality reached a turning point. The impetus for a new sexual politics was the antipornography movement, a movement committed to a particular critique of patriarchal sexuality." Emerging as part of increased feminist activism against many forms of violence against women, the movement found a concerned audience. Other feminists, however, voiced concern about the tone and content of the antipornography literature—confrontation and name-calling followed. The debate culminated in the public confrontation at the Barnard conference. This introduction precedes papers from a forum called to consider why the split over feminist theory about sexuality happened at this time and what is the meaning of this split.

Friedman, Deb. "Feminist Perspective on Pornography." *Off Our Backs,* January 1979, 2–3.

Friedman presents an overview of the first feminist conference on pornography held in San Francisco, November 1978, organized by WAVPM. The goal of the conference organizers was "to deepen our analysis of pornography and its relation to our lives, share all the information available on the subject . . ., produce resolutions for a working unit on those issues, and . . . create effective strategies for new and on-going organizing." Successes and failures are reported. There were workshops on the effects of pornography, pornography and racism, defining pornography, and pornography and the First Amendment. Speakers and content are reported by Friedman.

Friedman, Deb, and Lois Yankowski. "Snuffing Sexual Violence." *Quest* 3, Fall 1976, 24–30.

A summary of several discussions held by the Feminist Alliance Against Rape on the depiction of sexual violence in the media: "In discussing specific tactics that could be used to combat the proliferation of sexual violence, we decided against working for new censorship laws." Some alternatives are to work to change the Federal

Communications Commission guidelines to include standards about violence toward women and to form a national alert system to focus attention on offensive programming and films. Finally, they conclude, "The best general, long-term strategy is re-education."

Fritz, Leah. "Pornography as Gynocidal Propaganda." *New York University Review of Law and Social Change* 8, 1978–1979, 219–223.

Fritz writes that some relate pornography to sexual freedom and are alarmed that an effort to suppress it will end the new "liberation." Describes her experience as the writer of the "womens page" for *Screw,* and why she stopped. She details the war against women and how feminists must stop it. She says no minority group would stand for such demeaning portrayals of its sacred humanity. Fritz says, "Far from destroying the first amendment, conscious women will describe its limits—and thus make it less a hypocritical gesture."

Frye, Marilyn. "Provocative Positions." *The Women's Review of Books* 2, August 1985, 5–6.

A lengthy review of Joanna Russ's *Magic Mommas, Trembling Sisters, Puritans and Perverts,* which is an entry in this book. Frye says the essays collected in the book reviewed were very useful to her in helping to think about the sex versus pornography issues and feminist reporting of them.

Gardner, Frieda. "Getting Past the Censor." *The Women's Review of Books,* 3 May 1986, 9–10.

This is a lengthy review of *Women Against Censorship* edited by Varda Burstyn (Vancouver, B.C.: Douglas and MacIntyre, 1985). Gardner says "This is a partisan book, designed to grapple with the immediate and long term dangers posed by feminist proposals to combat pornography through the intervention of the state." Information and criticism of the workings of U. S. Attorney General Meese's Commission on Pornography are detailed by Gardner.

Garry, Ann. "Pornography and Respect for Women." *Social Theory and Practice* 4, Spring 1978, 395–421.

Describes the conflict between not wanting to control or censor the sexual and not wanting to degrade people, "especially women and others who are especially susceptible to it." The author attempts to resolve the conflict by considering these questions: Does pornography degrade human beings? Does it degrade women in ways that it does not degrade men? If so, must it degrade women? Garry argues that "although today much pornography does degrade women, it would be possible to have nondegrading, nonsexist pornography. However, this possibility rests on making certain fundamental changes in our conceptions of sex and sex role."

"German Feminism Discussed." *Off Our Backs,* October 1982, 8–10.

An interview by Carol Anne Douglas of *Off Our Backs,* with Sibylle Plogstedt, one of the editors of *Courage,* a feminist magazine from the Federal Republic of Germany. One of the topics of the interview is pornography. Sibylle Plogstedt says that advertising in Germany is getting more violent and that there is "some fighting about pornography in Germany," especially against peep shows. "The feminist movement is split on this issue. One group says that women earn a lot in these places. . . ." There have been demonstrations and other actions against pornographic publications. Sibylle is opposed to asking for laws against pornography.

Glastonbury, Marion. "At the Mercy of Men's Dreams." *New Statesman* 102, 6 November 1981, 18–19.

The author argues that the belief that women enjoy pain and submission is nonsense, that "pornography not only blames, punishes, and distorts women but also denies the possibilities of sexual pleasure." She cites titles, included here in the "Books" section, by two women, Beatrice Faust *(Women, Sex, and Pornography)* and Angela Carter *(The Sadeian Woman),* who "manage to feel at home in Bluebeard's castle." She notes that "During the hunt for the Yorkshire Ripper, a local cinema featuring *Violation of the Bitch* was picketed by eleven protesters. Police found time to arrest them."

Gordon, John. "Women Against Sex." *Playboy,* October 1980, 60–63.

In the introduction to the article there is the *Playboy* statement that Women Against Pornography and similar groups "believe that all erotic images are propaganda, part of a universal campaign against women." This author, John Gordon, takes "another view of the new enemies of eros." He says that the "Women Against Porn crusade suffers from confusion. It seems to be as much against sex as against sexist pornography." His article is a report of "an annual binge of funded dumbness called 'Women's Energy Weekend' where Women Against Pornography gave a presentation."

Gowens, Pat. "Porn, Poverty, Battery and the Feminist
    Movement." *Lesbian Contradictions*, Fall 1986, 17–18.
    The author offers an analysis of the popular beliefs surrounding male violence against women, especially the one that motivates the feminists antipornography movement: that violent sexual images turn men on and lead directly to violent sexual acts. Gowens says the real cause of violence is not sexual but the demand for power: "he gets his way; he gets revenge; he gets maid service; he gets real control. . . ." She believes "We must leave psycho-babble and middle-class arrogance and porn smoke-screens behind us." Women must unite together to use their power to stop the violence against them and not spend so much energy on worrying and organizing about alleged causes of the violence.

Gray, Susan H. "Exposure to Pornography and Aggression Toward
    Women: The Case of the Angry Male." *Social Problems* 29,
    April 1982, 387–398.
    States that the differing ideological positions on pornography, some of which are briefly noted here, have encouraged researchers to study what harmful effects, if any, result from pornography. This paper reviews the research done since 1970 into the effects of pornography on men's treatment of, and underlying attitudes to-ward, women. Gray interprets the results and her understanding of them. (See the annotation in the "Books" section under Klein, Freada, "Violence Against Women" for a reference to a criticism of Gray's analysis of what the research says.) Extensive references follow the article for the reader who wishes to study the research.

Griffin, Susan. "On Pornography." *Chrysalis* 1, c.1977, 15–17.
    "I am writing a series of journal entries. This may be one of them. They all belong to a book I will call *Pornography and Silence*." She then recounts the ways in which women have been silenced

through the centuries, and she considers freedom of speech—for men.

Guma, Greg, and Jo Schneiderman. "Women Campaign Against Pornography." *WIN,* 11 October 1979, 4–8.
    Report of some direct attacks on pornography shops, thoughts on "correct measures" to be taken against the proliferation of violent pornography "aimed at the brutal domination of women." Susan Brownmiller and Tillie Olsen are quoted as saying "The parallel rise of porn and the women's movement is evidence of an institutionalized counterrevolution."

Harrison, Barbara Grizzuti. "The Private Eye: This Column Is X-Rated." *Mademoiselle,* September 1984, 98.
    This writer says that attempts to control pornography won't work. She feels that the Indianapolis ordinance, which she describes, is too indefinite and would allow unsubstantial complaints. She fears its use against works not approved by the Moral Majority, and she believes it would be better to attack the disease and not pornography, which is only the symptom of the need to force sex and violence upon women.

Hartsock, Nancy. "Gender and Sexuality: Masculinity, Violence and Domination." *Humanities in Society* 7, Winter–Spring 1984, 19–45.
    It is argued that Western culture has interpreted human sexuality from the male perspective which, in turn, has been regularly viewed as an aggressive behavior motivated by the desire to dominate. Robert Stoller has maintained (*Sexual Excitement: The Dynamics of Erotic Life,* New York: Pantheon, 1979) that hostility is essential to sexual excitement and that sadistic behavior can come from women as well as men. Criticism of Stoller's work by Andrea Dworkin and other feminist critics is reviewed. In constructing a female sexuality that emphasizes alternatives to violence, other theories are explored.

Hawkes, Ellen. "Feminist Self-Destruction." *Penthouse,* October 1986, 94–95, 157.
    Hawkes is distressed by the divisiveness of the pornography issue among feminists. She does not agree with Andrea Dworkin or

her tactics. "Then Dworkin proceeds with racking sobs, to her litany of crimes against women supposedly caused by pornography . . . and I find her language as offensive as the most scurrilous smut." Hawkes believes that the arguments on pornography are basically about "how we, as women, choose to see ourselves." She feels the female-as-victim stance of the feminist antipornographers "assumes that women have no identities except those imposed by male stereotypes." She believes women are doing themselves a disservice by focusing on this issue "at a time when we are losing ground in the face of Reagan's social and economic policies."

Haygood, Griselda. "Mending Feminist Fences: Susan Brownmiller Answers Critics." *Womanews* (New York), April 1984, 15, 18.
An interview with Brownmiller which questions her about being accused of homophobia, racism, elitism, and other politically incorrect behavior. Includes information on a meeting of Women Against Pornography, a group which she helped to start.

Henry, Alice. "MacKinnon on Defining Pornography." *Off Our Backs*, June 1984, 14–15.
In an interview with Alice Henry, Catharine MacKinnon explains why pornography was defined in the terms which were used in the Minneapolis civil rights code proposed by herself and Andrea Dworkin. MacKinnon thinks that making pornography a violation of women's civil rights might be a move toward eliminating pornography, rather than merely pushing it underground. She says the word "subordination" was very deliberately chosen. Her reasoning behind the choice of language is detailed.

Henry, Alice. "Porn is Subordination?" *Off Our Backs*, November 1984, 20, 24.
The author looks at the language of the Minneapolis antipornography ordinance and says it was chosen to make it fit into a civil rights code. Ms. Henry poses the question: "Should speech, or ideology, be considered a discriminatory practice? In the U.S. . . . freedom of speech has been considered a very important principle." She also looks at the current research of Malamuth and Donnerstein. Two pages of back-and-forth commentary follow the article. Alice Henry does not believe that the scientific studies of the effects of pornography "say what some say they say," and that nothing yet is

proved. Many letters appeared in following *Off Our Backs* issues; see particularly February 1985, 25–27 under the title "Pornography, the Law, the Laboratory."

Herman, Sondra R. "Sex-Roles and Sexual Attitudes in Sweden: The New Phase." *The Massachusetts Review,* 13, Winter–Spring 1972, 45–64.

A historical overview is presented of the roles of and attitudes toward women in Sweden from the late nineteenth century on. Ironically, the Swedish tradition of patriarchal and active government has been the largest factor in women's drive for equality. The Swedes now receive official or semiofficial guidance in virtually every aspect of the sex question. The open discussion of sexuality and sexual rights is related to the challenge of the double standard by feminists and to man's proprietorship of women. The practice of discussing sexual matters frankly and realistically in mixed classes of boys and girls has eased the crisis of teenage pregnancies and venereal disease. Pornography is legal in Sweden and freely available, but feminists are now attacking it.

Hertzberg, Hendrik. "Big Boobs: Ed Meese and His Pornography Commission." *Harpers,* 195, 14 and 21 July 1986, 21–24.

In comparing the Meese Commission with the 1970 federal Commission on Obscenity and Pornography Hertzberg writes: "If the old commission was the federal equivalent of *Playboy,* the new one is the equivalent of *Hustler*—low budget, weak on fact-checking, unsubtle, and fascinated by the perverse." He reviews the composition of the commission, the witnesses it heard, and some of the "slippery reasoning" in its final report. He does not believe the report will spark a national crusade—largely because the sound defeat of the obscenity vote in Maine proves it is not a great political issue. The report will, however, "play an important part in a decentralized but wider effort to constrict personal liberty and freedom of expression."

Hirschberg, Lynn. "Brian DePalma's Death Wish." *Esquire,* January 1984, 79–83.

An interview with director Brian DePalma. His previous movies and present project, *Scarface,* are discussed, as well as the use of violence in his films. DePalma says, "To me, violence is just a visual form." His next project, *Body Double,* is also mentioned. DePalma says of it: "They wanna see suspense, they wanna see terror, they wanna see SEX—I'm the person for the job. It's going to be unbelievable."

For a reaction to this article see Joyce Sunila Holt's "DePalma's Rage to Sow a Porn Plot." *Los Angeles Times,* 4 March 1984, 37 in the "Newspapers" section below.

Hoagland, Sarah Lucia. "Violence, Victimization, Violation."
   Sinister Wisdom, issue 15, Fall 1980, 70–72.

The author believes that focusing on pornography with its depiction of violence against women and even focusing on rape as an act of violence is too narrow and short sighted. She says this only tempts us to turn to "male protection." She says if "we focus on the objectification and victimization of women," rather than specific acts or presentations, "it becomes clear that rape and porn together with protection are tools men use to enforce female heterosexuality."

Holz, Maxine. "Porn, Turn On or Put Down: Some Thoughts on
   Sexuality." *Processed World,* no. 7, Spring 1983, 38–52.

Holz disagrees with the antipornography arguments of Women Against Violence and Pornography in Media. She focuses her discussion on the movie *Not a Love Story,* "whose arguments are typical of the WAVPM campaign. . . ." She criticizes the film for heavily relying on "indignation and disgust that graphic sexual images tend to evoke." She questions the experts who are interviewed in the film. In addition, she feels the film's treatment of workers in the pornography industry "turns out to be heavily laced with a condescending, accusatory self-righteousness." While not uncritical of the sexism in pornography, Holz would not dismiss it as the antipornography feminists do. "The problem with both 'left' and 'right' antiporn campaigns is that they seek easy targets and unambiguous solutions, and exploit the high emotional voltage with which social taboos have charged the issue of sexuality."

Hommel, Teresa. "Images of Women in Pornography and Media."
   New York University Review of Law and Social Change, 8,
   1978–1979, 207–214.

Remarks and a slide presentation that accompanied them based upon a show prepared by Women Against Violence in Pornography and Media. Calls attention to repeated association of violence with sex and to the degradation of women. The author says the images of women as represented by pornography must be destroyed and that "feminists are working to humanize both the images and the roles of women and men in our society." She says it is time for men to reclaim masculine sexuality from the pornographers.

Hossie, Linda. "Jancis Andrews: Antiporn Activist." *Chatelaine*,
    September 1983, 63, 187–188, 190–194.
    This article is a portrait of a Vancouver, British Columbia woman described as a radical feminist and one of the most-active members of the antipornography crusade in Canada and a public speaker for its goals. Her work has focused on hard-core video stores in Canada. She has been successful in organizing women's groups to bring pressure to enforce provincial obscenity laws and to promote legislation. She wants various existing laws against hate literature to be used on behalf of women too.

Hughes, Patricia. "Pornography: Alternatives to Censorship."
    Canadian Journal of Political and Social Theory 9,
    Winter–Spring 1985, 96–126.
    A major element in the feminist analysis of pornography has been the appropriateness of censorship as a method of confronting pornographic materials. Arguing against censorship in its direct form, the author suggests other methods of reducing or counteracting pornography, and in general supports a human rights approach. Although the focus is primarily on pornography involving women, the analysis applies to homosexual and child pornography as well. Pornography is defined as coupling sex and violence or compulsion (or humiliation) into representations that serve as a tool of patriarchal ideology. Thus, it is a political rather than moral phenomenon. A discussion of the functions performed by pornography include the view that it constitutes a supporting pillar of patriarchy and male revenge for female sexuality, and it is a means by which males can attempt to control female sexuality, which they both fear and envy because it is associated with creation. Ways of dealing with pornography are considered, including self-help, municipal bylaws, criminal code prohibitions, and consecutive penalties. Two Canadian court

cases that have taken a feminist view of pornography are examined in detail.

Humes, Alison. "Fear of Porn—What's Really Behind It? An
    Interview with Carol S. Vance." *Vogue,* September 1985,
    679–680, 752.
    Vance is an anthropologist and epidemiologist at Columbia University, codirector of the Institute for the Study of Sex in Society and History, and a member of FACT. She does not believe pornography is dangerous for women, although she readily admits it is often sexist. She is concerned that the women's movement has continued to narrow its concerns with female sexuality to the current point of being focused on pornography, "as if pornography represented the locus of sexism in our culture. I don't see that it does." She is opposed to the ordinance restricting pornography because it reasserts that women are sexually different from men and in need of special protection. "Yet special protection inadvertently reinforces the ways in which women are legally and socially said to be different from men."

Hunter, Nan. "Sex-Baiting and Dangerous Bedfellows." *Off Our
    Backs,* July 1985, 33.
    A letter in which the writer, a well-known feminist who disagrees with the antipornography movement, wants to "separate those aspects of this debate which are vicious and destructive from those which are vital, important, and difficult but necessary." Hunter believes that the "sex baiting" and name calling at FACT members has been the low point of the debate. She details the accusations made against FACT supporters. She then goes on to consider the dangers of making alliances with right-wing people for any political reason. There are other letters about pornography on the same page, and responses in the *Off Our Backs* letters column in the December 1985 issue, page 27.

"Indy Anti-Porn Law Stalled." *Off Our Backs,* June 1984, 15.
    News report on the status of the Indianapolis ordinance that would ban sexually explicit, violent pornography. The law, signed into effect by Indianapolis Mayor William Hudnut on 1 May 1984 was awaiting its first test. U.S. District Court Judge Sarah Evans

Barker had issued a preliminary injunction barring enforcement of the ordinance until the legal and constitutional issues surrounding it could be resolved.

Jacobs, Caryn. "Patterns of Violence: A Feminist Perspective on the Regulation of Pornography." *Harvard Women's Law Journal* 7, Spring 1984, 5–55.

The first part of the article explains why pornography is a women's issue. It includes evidence of pornography's link to violence, its vision of women and sexuality, its harm to women. Jacobs states that feminists reject the attempts to repress sexual knowledge and sexual freedom by traditional opponents of pornography; they also reject the liberal view that all pornography should be unrestricted regardless of content. Part II of the article deals with pornography and the First Amendment. Part III is entitled "Regulating Pornography Under a Feminist Standard." Footnotes provide numerous references to articles and law cases. Especially useful are the citations of critiques and studies of the *Presidents' Commission on Obscenity and Pornography Reports* (1970).

Jaehne, Karen. "Confessions of a Feminist Porn Programmer." *Film Quarterly* 37, Fall 1983, 9–16.

Jaehne writes about her experiences as a film programmer for a late-night cable television "adult" program. She describes what standards were applied—both by the television station administration and the FCC. She discusses soft porn as a genre and how it is changing to appeal to a larger female audience and by the work of female directors. "Meanwhile, the dangers of over-reacting to the idea of pornography lead to accusations and counter-accusations among feminists, as Ruby Rich has warned; feminism ought to be able to discuss the issues of pornography without dismissing the importance of sexuality."

Johnson, Hillary. "Violence Against Women—Is Porn to Blame?" *Vogue,* September 1985, 678–679, 750–752.

A survey of the current research on the effects of pornography on male behavior. Studies by Neil Malamuth at the University of California at Los Angeles are described, as well as studies on the rise in violent, sadistic pornography. "Malamuth stresses that violent pornography's proven area of influence has been in reinforcing aggressive attitudes among men: actual violence is a result of a complicated set of interactions." Lawyers and feminists are closely following these studies, says Johnson.

Kaminer, Wendy. "A Woman's Guide to Pornography and the Law." *The Nation*, 21 June 1980, 754–756.
Legal processes and principles make laws against pornography "difficult to pass, and dangerous to free speech." The author says feminists should not advocate censorship but have the right to protest material degrading to women. She points out that "trashing a porn shop" may be an offense but it does not violate the First Amendment.

Kaufman, Gloria. "S/M and Porn Touch Issues For The Movement." *New Directions for Women*, September–October 1982, 4.
Kaufman is concerned that the issues of sadomasochism and pornography are diverting the feminist movement from other goals. "It may be, after much discussion that feminists will continue to disagree on the pornography issue. (Perhaps that is the true import of the S/M phenomenon.) It is, however, much too early for hardened battlelines to be forming."

Kelly, Janis, and Fran Moira. "A Clear and Present Danger." *Off Our Backs*, January 1979, 7.
The article explains why pornography should be more, not less, visible. Definitions of pornography are so unclear they could be turned against anything. Freedom of speech is a prerequisite to any decent society we can envision. The authors say: "We should be making pornography more, not less, visible. One of the strongest supports male supremacy has, is the refusal of most women to believe that the degradation of women is central to male culture."

Killoran, M. Maureen. "Sticks and Stones Can Break My Bones and Images Can Hurt Me: Feminists and the Pornography Debate." *International Journal of Women's Studies* 6, November–December 1983, 443–456.
Contemporary feminist literature on pornography is reviewed and situated relative to liberal and conservative positions. Author says: "The traditional debate on pornography evolves around

whether sexuality is 'good' or 'bad.' Most feminists see pornography in the cultural context of the male/female domination/subordination hierarchy. . . ." The author believes feminists must pay greater attention to pornography as "a symptom of the misogynistic practices by which women are subordinated."

Kirkendall, Lester, Gina Allen, Albert Ellis, and Helen Colton. "Sex Magazines and Feminism." *Humanist,* November–December 1978, 44–51.

The authors argue in a symposium that pornography must be accepted as a part of human life and that authorities in sexual matters must disseminate their knowledge through popular or even pornographic magazines to reach audiences. The article notes that pornography can be life-affirming and not necessarily demeaning.

Kirkpatrick, R. George, and Louis A. Zurcher, Jr. "Women Against Pornography: Feminist Anti-Pornography Crusades in American Society." *The International Journal of Sociology and Social Policy* 3, 1983, 1–30.

A historical and theoretical analysis of antipornography campaigns over a ten-year period, with a survey of thirty-five women leaders of feminist antipornography action. Characteristics of those women are examined including educational background, occupation, religion, age, rural-urban origin, income, politics, self-concept, and organizational links to antipornography groups. Respondents were administered a questionnaire regarding the goals of feminist antipornography organizations, movies and books judged to be pornographic, attitudes toward the producers and consumers of pornography, the relationship between pornography and violence, causes of child pornography, the difference between pornography and erotica, exposure to pornography as a child, and experience as a victim of sexual assault and rape. Social-psychological characteristics of feminist and Christian right-wing, antipornography crusaders were compared. Feminists are found to be very different from Christian right-wing, antipornography crusaders in both demographic and social-psychological variables. Several recent books in the feminist tradition attacking pornography as "the ideology of cultural sadism" and "male supremacist patriarchal rape culture" are reviewed, along with recent research on the relationship between viewing pornography and violent attitudes of men toward women.

Klapper, Zina. "Sex, Porn and Art Actions." *Mother Jones,* June 1981, 6.

Describes some of the actions against pornography by Preying Mantis Women's Brigade such as protest tableaus outside of films, pelting beauty pageant officials with ribbon-wrapped meat, and destroying issues of *Hustler* magazine. The brigade says it is opposed to government censorship and does not support the Moral Majority's call for the suppression of erotica.

Klein, Dorie. "Violence Against Women: Some Considerations Regarding Its Causes and Its Elimination." *Crime and Delinquency* 27, January 1981, 64–80.

Violence against women is identified as an outcome of the social structure and ideology of gender domination. Its very definition is related to changes in women's place in male-dominated society. Specific crimes against women are grouped and analyzed as originating in female subordination in the gender-specific arenas of reproduction, sexuality, and nurturance. Despite recent formal legal gains through decreased childbearing, and a male-oriented "sexual revolution," neither individual nor systemic violence against women has slackened. This is related to the fact that as traditional patriarchy appears to be replaced by the rule of the state, public institutions, and medicine over "personal" life, male domination is transformed rather than eroded. A qualitatively different development is the achievement of the feminist movement in exposing, defining, and challenging abuses of women. It is suggested that feminist strategies to use the criminal justice process to achieve liberation, as evidenced by legal reform movements with regard to pornography and family violence, should take into account the limitations of a structure of which predominant determinants are the protection of economic order and ideological legitimacy.

Klein, Jeffry. "Born Again Porn." *Mother Jones,* February–March 1978, 12–23.

Details of a trip and interview with *Hustler* publisher Larry Flynt and his beliefs about pornography, women and men, the First

Amendment, and his conversations on both his obscenity and conspiracy charges. His conversion to "Born-again Christianity" is reported as are, briefly, attitudes toward feminists. Staff people at the *Hustler* offices are also interviewed.

Kole, Janet. "Closing the Gender Gap—in Court." *Vogue,*
    December 1984, 194.
    Brief description of the efforts in Minneapolis and Indianapolis to ban the sale of pornography. Notes danger to the First Amendment, difficulty of definitions, the "alliance of feminists and the religious right."

Kolenda, Konstantin. "Porno Prone." *Humanist* 45, July–August
    1985, 45.
    Kolenda believes pornography is offensive because it ignores the Kantian principle called "the Categorical Imperative: always treat human beings as ends in themselves and never as means only." Treating people like objects makes it very easy for pornography to slide into violence. "Pornography and other forms of violence accept the immoral principle that it is all right to use people as means to gratuitous thrills."

Kostash, Myrna. "Power and Control: A Feminist View of
    Pornography." *This Magazine* 12, July–August 1978, 4–7.
    Comments on liberals' defense of the conviction of Larry Flynt, publisher of *Hustler* magazine. Kotash says he is not a victim but a trader in the degradation of women. "Flynt is no dissident: he is a pimp." She then describes how the women's movement requires and makes possible a new analysis of pornography and men's attraction to it. She makes it "clear that resistance to pornography is not the same as the desire to legislate sexuality."

Krauathammer, Charles. "Pornography Through the Looking
    Glass." *Time,* 12 March 1984, 82-83.
    Krauathammer likens the Minneapolis City Council, which recently passed an antipornography ordinance based on civil rights, to ". . . Alice's Wonderland, words will mean what the council wants them to mean." What he finds "audacious and perverse" about the Minneapolis bill is "It manages the amazing feat of restoring censor-

ship, which after all is a form of coercion, while at the same time claiming not to restrict rights but expand them." He can well understand why a community may want to curb pornography, but "why be so coy about giving censorship its proper name too."

Kraus, Hildie Verlaine. "Feminist Strippers Clash With Women
 Against Porn." *Plexus,* 12 September 1984, 1.
 Some views of women "in the sex industry" who speak out against the view that pornography degrades women and encourages violence against them. Sunlove, a producer of erotic performances, laments the image that women on stage are seen as helpless and exploited, that women in the sex industry are powerless and oppressed. She says, "I get very upset when women are depicted as so helpless, so naive . . . these women are self-determined, they made a choice to be in this business." Fanny Fatale, too, supports the views of Mistress Kat Sunlove. Ilze Betins, a feminist and leader of WOMBAT, a group opposed to pornography, does not agree that the sexual fantasies supported by sex industry workers are harmless. Betins claims that the women above are not reflective of all sex industry workers. This article quotes a radio debate on Station KSFO on 5 August 1984.

Lacayo, Richard. "Give-And-Take On Pornography." *Time,* 10
 March 1986, 67.
 Report on the U.S. Supreme Court's decision to uphold the federal appeals court ruling that the Indianapolis antipornography ordinance is unconstitutional. Catharine MacKinnon said of the decision: " 'Six men on the Supreme Court stood up for organized crime.' " Phyllis Schlafly commented: " 'It allows pornographers to clothe themselves in the First Amendment while they're undressing women.' " Lacayo also discusses the Supreme Court's decision upholding zoning ordinances for adult movie theaters.

Lacy, Suzanne. "Organizing: The Art of Protest." *Ms,* October
 1982, 67.
 The author, a performance artist based in Los Angeles, describes various street activities for organizing and political purposes. She includes a description of the march of 3,000 women participants

in the first National Feminist Perspectives on Pornography Conference.

Lahey, Kathleen A. "The Canadian Charter of Rights and
  Pornography." *New England Law Review* 20, 1984–1985,
  649–685.
  Lahey details the variety of personal reactions to pornography
and the resultant political differences between women. She "explores
several themes that have emerged in debates over pornography, state
regulation, and feminist theory." Finally she discusses "the legal
implications of the sex/gender equality provisions of the Canadian
Charter of Rights." (Canadian Constitution, amendment to Charter
of Rights and Freedoms, Ch. 11, Sched. B, 1–34 [1982]). She
concludes by challenging "the masculist analysis of the so-called
conflict between pornography and free speech" on a number of
fundamental points. She also asks, "How 'free' do women really
want to be? Do women want to challenge masculist dominance at
the levels of discourse, of legal analysis, of political strategy, and of
empowerment? Or does the emergence of the feminist antipornography movement in North America indicate that women have
begun to appease men. . . .?"

"Laura Lederer: Feminists Present a Third View of Pornography
  and First Amendment." *Media Report to Women*, 1 December
  1980, 6-7.
  A synopsis of some of the viewpoints of contributors to the
book *Take Back the Night: Women on Pornography*. There are excerpts
from Wendy Kaminer, Robin Yeamans, Susan Brownmiller, and
Andrea Dworkin. The same article has a brief note on Angela
Carter's *The Sadeian Woman* and some names and addresses of
antipornography women's groups. These titles are listed here under
"Books" section.

"The Left and Porno." *Cineaste* 7, Winter 1976–77, 28–31.
  The editors of *Cineaste* requested contributions on the topic "a
left viewpoint on pornography in general and porno films in particular." One of the suggested areas the essays might cover was: "Many
feminists feel that porno films are *inherently* sexist. What do you
think?"

James Monaco, contributing editor of *More (The Media Magazine),* agreed with that statement. "It's interesting to note, as well, that women are generally not much less exploited in non-porn films in this country." Poet Susan Sherman writes: "To oppose pornography is not to oppose liberty, it is to oppose the objectification of oppression. It is to oppose an *educative* tool, an indoctrination technique of an oppressive, sexist society." Julia Lesage, associate editor for *Jump Cut,* criticizes the question. "But *Cineaste's* only reference to a feminist perspective on porn is one that makes it easy to reject, for the question is stated in ahistorical terms about the essence of porn."

Replies from Todd Gitlin, Lee Baxandall, and Ernest Callenbach are also printed.

Leidholdt, Dorchen. "Stripper and Director Merge in Porn Film." *New Directions for Women,* September–October 1982, 18.
A review of the feminist documentary, *Not A Love Story.* Leidholdt praises the film for showing "how the hatred of women that is pornography's essential content circumscribes the lives of both the women inside the sex supermarkets and the feminists who picket outside." Despite a few flaws in the film, she urges readers to see it and "to take all your liberal friends who insist that pornography is harmless fantasy."

Leidholdt, Dorchen. "Where Pornography Meets Fascism." *WIN,* 15 March 1983, 18–22.
Dorchen, a founder and active member of Women Against Pornography, describes examples of pornography from current magazines and paintings and compares them with the work of Franz von Stuch, Hitler's favorite artist. She believes that this is not an accident and that it is because there are "pronounced ideological similarities" between them. "At the core of both pornography and fascism is biological determinism." She goes on to document her case with details of similarity. "Biological determinism is inherent not just in pornography's conception of women in general, but in its depiction of minority women in particular. In pornography, all of the culture's racist myths become just another turn-on." She feels the liberal left has been indifferent to this racism.

Leidholdt, Dorchen, and Florence Rush. "Pro-Law Women Blast
   Their Critics." *New Directions for Women,* January-February
   1985, 12.

Leidholdt, cofounder of Women Against Pornography, and
Rush, author of *The Best Kept Secret: Sexual Abuse of Children,* are
extremely critical of the Feminist Anti-Censorship Task Force that
opposes antipornography legislation. They believe these women
deny the power and size of the pornography industry, as well as its
violence. "At the root of the arguments presented by the legislation's
critics is a refusal to confront the reality of pornography."

Leo, John. "Pornography: The Feminist Dilemma." *Time,* 21 July
   1986, 18.

A review of various feminists' reaction to the Meese Commission report. Some see it as "good for the women's movement (law
professor Catharine MacKinnon), bad for the movement (ACLU
attorney Nan Hunter), or basically irrelevant to feminist issues
(movement pioneer Betty Friedan)." Includes a brief review of the
MacKinnon-Dworkin antiporn legislation, and its feminist supporters and opponents.

Leonard, Vickie. "Women's Porn?" *Off Our Back* ;, April 1983, 5,
   12.

Report of a panel discussion at the Women and Movies III
Conference in Washington, D.C. The speakers were Jean Callahan of
American Film Magazine, Gloria Leonard of *High Society,* a sexually
explicit magazine, Ruby Rich, a feminist film critic and Elizabeth
Hess, moderator. The panel and the audience discussion that followed "seemed to establish, with notable exceptions that: women
primarily enjoy the same sexual activities that men do, sex is on the
rise everywhere in film and video, women have been deprived of
seeing [that] with which they could identify. . . . The possibility that
pornography is intrinsically anti-woman was never directly addressed." Gloria Leonard lamented that feminists never supported
her as a successful woman breaking into a man's field and pointed
out that the sex industry had created a lot of jobs for women. Ruby
Rich spoke about feminists working against pornography.

"Letters . . . Responding to the Barnard Conference on Sexuality."
Off Our Backs, August–September 1982, 32–33.
Many comments and commentary on the conference, the coverage of, and responses to the conference. Letters by Claudette Charbonneau, Ellen Willis, and Joan Nestle mention the antipornography activists in one context or another.

Lindsay, Karen. "Brownmiller on Feminity and Pornography."
Sojourner, May 1985, 24–25.
An interview with Susan Brownmiller which includes her
thoughts on the antipornography movement, which she supports.
However, Brownmiller believes the MacKinnon-Dworkin ordinance
is too vague, that the association with fundamentalists "has got to be
enlightening to them" and that "pornography has gotten out-of-
hand" and "something will be done to curtail it."

Lord, Lisi. "Porn and the Mind." *Aegis: Magazine on Ending
Violence Against Women,* no. 37, 1983, 21.
The prevalence of pornography in our society is due to the
demand for it from consumers. The author says pornography is a
symptom of a much larger problem in our culture. She says, "In
order to show that pornography's themes prevail throughout our
society this paper will draw parallels between the pornography
industry and another major institution in our society, the military."
She discusses both pornography and the military as male institutions
and how both require the domination of women. She concludes that
the parallels exist, "and in fact these institutions exist because of
men's need, socialized into them from birth, to dominate others
different from themselves."

"Lynch Gives ALA Views to Pornography Panel." *American
Libraries,* October 1985, 607–608.
Testimony before the U.S. Attorney General's Commission on
Pornography at its 24–25 June 1985 hearings in Chicago. The topic
at these particular hearings was "Law Enforcement Initiatives."
American Library Association president, Beverly Lynch, urged the
commissioners "not to recommend any further controls on access to
materials of any kind, indeed, to recommend elimination of any
restrictions that now exist."

Lynn, Barry W. " 'Civil Rights' Ordinances and the Attorney
    General's Commission: New Developments in Pornography
    Regulation." *Harvard Civil Rights—Civil Liberties Law Review*
    21, Winter 1986, 27–125.

Lynn, American Civil Liberties Union legislative counsel, begins this article with information on the "de facto coalition of
feminists and religious fundamentalists" in Indianapolis, Indiana
"which convinced the Mayor and City Council to pass an antipornography ordinance." He then turns to the U.S. Attorney General's
Commission on Pornography and lists of its members and their
affiliations. After this introduction, the article "first examines the
current content and legal status of sexually-explicit material and then
takes a hard look at the allegedly new arguments and evidence which
have been offered to justify suppression of that material." There are
many references to cases, articles and other commentary in the
extensive notes. The author concludes by saying that "neither those
who support the 'sex discrimination' ordinances, nor those more
traditional pornography opponents who have endorsed the new
commission, have advanced principles acceptable to a society that is
truly supportive of free expression and personal privacy."

McCarthy, Sarah J. "Pornography, Rape, and the Cult of Macho."
    The Humanist 40, September–October 1980, 11–20.

She says that to ignore pornography as being simply male
fantasy is to ignore research on the role of the socialization process in
shaping behavior. Various experiments in behavior modification are
described together with what McCarthy believes they tell us about
influences on people and about the need for education. "One of the
primary purposes of feminists against pornography is to educate
women and men who do not usually read porn." Details on Women
Against Pornography, studies on sex and violence, and attitudes of
women are included.

McCormack, Thelma. "Machismo in Media Research: A Critical
    Review of Research on Violence and Pornography." *Social
    Problems* 25, June 1978, 552–554.

Two areas of media research, violence and pornography, as
studied by Causes and Prevention of Violence (1969), the Commission on Obscenity and Pornography (1970), and the Surgeon
General's Report on Television and Social Behavior (1972), are

examined for an explanation of their "discrepant findings." The author says that these research studies are characterized by sexist biases. She notes that feminists have been critical of this research. She suggests that the underlying reason for the discrepancy is a machismo orientation defined as a narcissistic pride in sexual virility (pornography), the other side of which is anxiety about male sexual identity. Also, "the instruments used by the investigators perpetrate the myth of female sexual passivity." She proposes ways in which some sociological theory (reference group theory and F-scale research) can eliminate bias.

McDaniel, Ann. "A Salvo in the Porn War." *Newsweek,* 21 July
    1986, 18.
    News story on the release of the Meese Commission on Pornography report. Includes brief descriptions of the commission's recommendations, and the increased activity around the country against pornographic materials, such as the conviction of a southern California X–rated film producer.

McDonald, Lynn. "Censorship and the New Pornography." *The
    Canadian Forum,* May 1983, 36–37.
    The author calls the "new pornography" brutal and says that there is no way to avoid seeing it because it's everywhere including "the corner store." McDonald describes some rape scenes and other scenes of violence on video and says other groups—other than women—would not allow themselves to be objectified or degraded in this manner. She believes films and other visual images of sex and violence toward women may indeed be dangerous. "No one wants to impede the publication of words but yes, some of us do want to stop the broadcasting, and other dissemination, of certain degrading and, especially violent images." McDonald writes about Canadian broadcasting regulations, licenses for pay-TV companies, and the other Canadian laws. McDonald is a Member of Parliament. For a lengthy reply to her opinions see Jimmy Manson's "Pornography and Feminism," *Canadian Forum,* December, 1983.

McDonald, Lynn, and Jimmy Manson. "Pornography and
    Feminism." *The Canadian Forum,* December 1983, 5–6.
    Manson criticizes McDonald's article in the May 1983 issue of
Canadian Forum for making the question of censorship the main

issue in the debate on pornography and in doing so having neglected "to undertake a comprehensive and responsible study of pornography and its alleged effects." He goes on to attempt to discredit all the arguments of the antipornography activists.

This is followed by a lengthy reply from McDonald which concludes, "Denounce pornography."

MacKinnon, Catharine A. "Not a Moral Issue." *Yale Law and Policy Review* 2, Spring 1984, 321–345.

Feminist legal critique of pornography, and the "abstract approach to freedom of speech embodied in First Amendment doctrine." Author says that "the pornographer's lawyers have persuasively presented First Amendment absolutism, their advocacy position, as a legal fact, which it has never been." In her essay MacKinnon makes a distinction between obscenity and pornography. The next issue of *Yale Law and Policy Review* (3, 1984) contained a response to this article: Thomas I. Emerson's "Pornography and The First Amendment: A Reply to Professor MacKinnon."

MacKinnon, Catharine A. "Pornography, Civil Rights, and Speech." *Harvard Civil Rights—Civil Liberties Law Review* 20, Winter 1985, 1–70.

MacKinnon, law professor and coauthor with Andrea Dworkin of an ordinance defining pornography as a civil rights violation, here presents the theoretical basis for her position. The premise is that "pornography is central in creating and maintaining the civil inequality of the sexes."

MacKinnon, Catharine. "Take Porn Money and . . ." *Off Our Backs*, October 1982, 5.

Report of a talk presented at the National Women's Studies Association conference called "On Playboy's Money: A Feminist Perspective" where she stressed her desire for confrontation of her views. She saw two positions on taking *Playboy*'s money. One, "that it's our money anyway" and should be taken to destroy the system and two, "that taking *Playboy*'s money digs us deeper into the system we are fighting." *Playboy,* she said, "is pornography and that pornography is the ideology of male supremacy. It legitimizes forced sex."

MacKinnon wants to "delegitimate pornography, including *Playboy."*
She said that *"Playboy* legitimizes pornography, and that *Playboy* is
legitimized in many ways including printing articles by feminists—
and by feminists taking *Playboy*'s money and *Playboy* advertising
that." MacKinnon ended her talk with many questions, and there
followed a "vigorous exchange with the audience."

Mahoney, Kathleen E. "Obscenity, Morals and the Law: A
    Feminist Critique." *Ottawa Law Review* 17, November 1984,
    33–71.
    Mahoney's premise is that men and women have a different
conception of morality and justice. She draws from the work of
psychologist Carol Gilligan who found men have a hierarchical view
of morality ("The metaphor for men is the ladder"), while women
define their moral judgments in terms of their relationships to others
("The metaphor for women is the web"). Noting that until recently
law was written and interpreted by men, she looks at how the issues
of obscenity and pornography are being altered by women's interpretation of the law based on their different sense of morality. She
concludes: "A number of laws have been altered in recent years in
recognition of the fact that the law has not recognized women's
interests fairly in the past. Obscenity laws should also change, for in
their present state they are outdated and unacceptable."
    Many references, most to Canadian legal sources.

Malamuth, Neil M., and James V.P. Check. "Effects of Mass Media
    Exposure on Acceptance of Violence Against Women." *Journal
    of Research in Personality* 15, December 1981, 436–446.
    Two hundred seventy-one male and female students served as
subjects in an experiment on the effects of exposure to films that
portray sexual violence as having positive consequences. Details of
the methodology, setting, and control for the experiment are presented in detail. The results indicated that exposure to the films
portraying violent sexuality increased male subjects' acceptance of
interpersonal violence against women. Different results were found
for females. Research report is included here because of frequent
citation.

Malamuth, Neil M., Seymour Feshbach, and Yoram Jaffee. "Sexual
    Arousal and Aggression: Recent Experiments and Theoretical
    Issues." *Journal of Social Issues* 33, Spring 1977, 110–133.
    Authors note that recent studies have found that under different
experimental conditions there are both facilitative and inverse relationships between sex and aggression. They believe this may be
explained by incorporating in future studies distinctions between
hostile and assertive aggression. There are extensive references to
scientific studies. They note, in this article, that much of pornography is "hostile aggressivity."

Manson, Jimmy. "Pornography and Feminism." *Canadian Forum,*
    [Letters] December 1983, 5–6.
    A lengthy response to "Censorship and the New Pornography"
(see Lynn McDonald) in which Manson accuses the antipornography crusaders and the civil libertarians of neglecting serious study
of the alleged effects of pornography. Further he claims that the
"virulently 'anti-porn' feminists" have overemphasized the violence
against women in pornography and that close monitoring of the
"Adult Film Industry" indicates "that ninety-two percent of the
feature films now being shown are of the 'garden variety,' silly, yet
innocuous and non-violent depictions of carnal escapades." He goes
on to attempt to discredit most other attacks on pornography and
ends by explaining the movement by saying it is simply prudish. This
is followed by a reply from Lynn McDonald who says she knows of
no antipornography feminists who don't make the distinction between sex and violence. And she continues, "Nor will his calling antipornography activists names discourage us from the task."

Mead, Margaret. "Women and the 'New' Pornography." *Redbook,*
    February 1976, 29–32.
    Mead comments on the new marketing of pornography to the
modern, sexually liberated woman and discusses what this "current
blossoming forth" of pornography may mean.

"Media." *Playboy,* October 1980, 30.
    The author of this column takes exception to Dr. Joyce Brothers
who advised a reader, who had been criticized for joining a women's
group that was fighting pornography, that "most pornography
involves acts that are sadistic—usually toward a woman or some-

times a child. This is neither good nor healthy. It is destructive to both the victim and the victimizer." The author of "Media" disagrees with Dr. Brothers, and says why.

Melendy, Suzanne. "Massachusetts Anti-Porno Legislation."
Womanews (New York City), February 1986, 9.
Report of the Cambridge, Massachusetts voters defeat of a referendum question which would have amended the city's human rights ordinance to define pornography as a form of sex discrimination. The amendment, written by Andrea Dworkin and Catharine MacKinnon, defined pornography as a civil rights violation. The 5 November 1985 vote in Cambridge marked the first time such a law has appeared as a municipal ballot question.

Mills, Stephanie. "Feminism and Pornography." *CoEvolution Quarterly,* Spring, 1982, 1.
Mills says that reading pornography can be a turn-on, but at the same time "my absorption in the paradoxical fantasy of pleasurable rape had overridden my identification with the pain of the women being violated. The arousal was a betrayal of self." The author believes that one must accept without question the sexual choices of consenting adults. "But antipornography efforts have convinced me that many women find themselves victimized. . . . I do not buy the idea that . . . violent pornography is harmless: it is propaganda for rape."

"Minneapolis Anti-Porn Ordinance." *Off Our Backs,*
August–September 1984, 5.
Report on the status of the Minneapolis controversial anti-pornography ordinance. At the time of the writing of this news report, the city council had passed the ordinance by a seven-to-six vote in June, and Mayor Donald Fraser had vetoed it. Ordinance supporters were attempting to get enough city council support to override the veto.

"Minneapolis: Critical Condition." *Off Our Backs,*
August–September 1984, 5.
Ruth Christensen, who set fire to herself in a Minneapolis bookstore to protest the degradation of women by pornographers, was in critical condition but expected to live. She had sent copies of a

four-page suicide note to members of the city council saying that she hoped they would pass the civil rights legislation before them.

"Minneapolis Porn Ordinance." *Off Our Backs,* January 1984, 1–2.
A report on the Minneapolis City Council's consideration of a proposal to amend its civil rights ordinance to include pornography as an act of sex discrimination. Under contract through the city attorney's office, feminist lawyer and professor, Catharine A. Mac-Kinnon, and feminist writer, Andrea Dworkin, drafted the amendment which the city council passed by a vote of seven-to-six. The history of the veto by Mayor Donald Fraser and the appointment of a task force to study and make recommendations are reported.

Morgan, Robin. "How to Run the Pornographers Out of Town (and Preserve the First Amendment)." *Ms,* November 1978, 55–80.
A report on the growing resistence to pornography. Morgan notes that she was first jailed in a feminist protest against pornography eight years ago, "but it took the intervening almost-decade for that issue to be admitted as a main concern of the women's movement." There is information on the pornography industry, feminist's response to escalating misogyny, studies on "causality." Morgan suggests some activities to make pornographers less comfortable.

Morgan, Robin. "The Sadeian Woman and the Ideology of Pornography." *New Republic,* 1 September 1979, 31–33.
See the entry under Carter, Angela, *The Sadeian Woman and the Ideology of Pornography,* in "Books" section of this bibliography.

Murray, Maureen. "Pornography Debate Saps Feminist Energy." *New Directions for Women,* September–October 1985, 10–11.
Delineates pro and con arguments of feminists regarding the antipornography ordinances. Notes especially the fear of involvement with the right wing, the ways in which the ordinances might be used against feminist issues, and the difficulty in distinguishing between erotica and pornography. Reports the government's formation of a commission to study the effects of pornography on behavior.

"Name-calling Deplored." *New Directions for Women,* July–August
    1982, 15.
    Reprints the petition that was circulated at the Barnard confer-
ence in response to statements made by the Coalition for a Feminist
Sexuality and Against Sadomasochism (Women Against Violence
Against Women, Women Against Pornography, New York Radical
Feminists). Also prints an excerpt from the coalition's protest of the
conference.

Neier, Aryeh. "Expurgating the First Amendment." *The Nation,* 21
    June 1980, 727, 751–754.
    The author notes a trend of oppressed groups willing to de-
mand censorship of materials they oppose. In other times, "free
speech was a rallying cry for the victims of oppression." He says
advocates of free speech must fight back, and those who call for
censorship, including feminists, must find a better strategy to combat oppression.

Neier, Aryeh. "Memoirs of a Woman's Displeasure." *The Nation,*
    16–23 August 1980, 1, 154–156.
    The author considers the attention given to Linda Lovelace and
her story of coercion in performing in pornography films, and
relates it to the view of "fallen women" during the last three
centuries. He says that by assuming that all women who take part in
pornography are forced to do so, feminists are aligning themselves
with the nineteenth-century belief that women were mere pawns in
the hands of men. He says that feminists aren't willing to admit some
women do this by choice. He concludes the article by saying, "No
doubt males have much to answer for, but it is not clear that the
feminist cause is advanced by insisting that any woman who exploits
her body is not responsible for her own life."
    For a response and a counterresponse to this article, see above
Mary Ellis Donovan, "Feminists and Porn." *The Nation,* 3–10
January 1981, 2, 20.

Nestle, Joan. "My History With Censorship." *Bad Attitudes* 1,
    Spring 1985, 2–4.
    Nestle describes the despair she feels "at the new antipornog-
raphy movement and the censorial atmosphere that is fed by it. . . ."
Nestle describes her own experiences and how disheartening it is to

encounter the same attitudes from feminists and lesbians that she had experienced from the House Un-American Activities Committee types of the fifties. She tells of late-night calls after the Barnard conference on sexuality and censorship of her own writings from women's publications and bookstores. She finishes by saying, "I almost think I have lived too long when I see lesbians become members of the new vice squads."

"New FACT Group Battles Censorship Laws." *New Directions for Women,* January–February 1985, 1, 13.

Brief mention of the first antipornography actions of women in 1976 followed by a recount of attempts to pass legislation in Minneapolis; Indianapolis; Suffolk County, New York; Madison, Wisconsin; St. Louis; Detroit; Los Angeles, and New York City. Then the formation of FACT in 1984 and its position on antipornography laws are reported in detail.

FACT sees such legislation as having a "chilling effect on expression," and that it could easily become a "building block for a larger protectionist document." The Suffolk County, New York, legislation is cited as an example of this. While they admit some pornography is insulting to women, "so are ads, situation comedies, and many women's magazines." They do not believe legislation is the answer. In fact, they conclude: "The current preoccupation with banning pornography diverts money and attention from programs and services that women really need, and create a false sense of security that something important is being done."

"Nikki Craft, Activist and Outlaw." *Off Our Backs,* July 1985, 1–7.

This is an interview by Tricia Lootens and Alice Henry with Nikki Craft. It details her background of activism, her committment to civil disobedience as political action, her involvement with the anti-rape movement and many details on specific actions taken by Craft and her supporters, a veritable "how-to-do-it" handbook. Craft describes her "Stack o' Wheats" action at the University of California, Santa Cruz, and her decision to use civil disobedience against pornography because "I don't trust the government to decide what we should be exposed to." She details more of her philosophy, the founding of the Preying Mantis Brigade, and various antipornography actions.

Omi, Michael. "We're Not Gonna Take It: Censorship Is Back."
   Socialist Review 16, January–February 1986, 123.
   Article about a number of historical incidents involving popular culture being singled out for its supposedly corrupting influence. Details are given on the pressures being brought to bear against the recording industry. Omi pointed out that one of the first campaigns to "clean up" the record companies "was initiated by parts of the feminist movement" when Women Against Violence Against Women defaced the Sunset Strip billboard advertising a Rolling Stones recording ("I'm 'Black and Blue' from the Rolling Stones—and I Love It!"). He notes other more recent and similar activities.

"On the Great Pornography Debate." *Ms,* July 1985, 8–12.
   Many letters—three pages worth—in response to the Mary Kay Blakely article "Is One Woman's Sexuality Another Woman's Pornography?", *Ms,* April 1985 (see above). A number of the letters raise substantive issues and observations on the feminist antipornography debate. Some congratulate *Ms* on a "breakthrough cover story" on "the other side of the debate." Other correspondents say "*Ms* has joined the ranks of pornographers."

Pally, Marcia. "Double Trouble." *Film Comment* 20,
   September–October 1984, 12–17.
   Pally prefaces her interview with Brian DePalma with very brief descriptions of some of the violent scenes in his films *Carrie, Dressed to Kill,* and *Body Double.* "To the folks in the antiporn movement, DePalma's images are up there on the screen inciting people to sin (the new right), or teaching violence against women (feminist antiporners)." She then gives a brief history of the feminist antipornography activities. Her interview with DePalma, among other topics, covers feminist antipornography activities, Vanessa Williams, the women's movement, capitalism, and the media.
   Palla asks DePalma what he thinks of the argument that links pornography and violence against women. He responds: "Makes no sense to me. I've seen a lot of movies and a lot of porn, and it's not made me violent to women in *any* way."
   On the general topic of who decides what is art and what is porn, DePalma says: "I think the antiporn movement is dealing with duplicitous arguments. They're worried about walking into one of

my films when in their neighborhoods there are stores selling pornographic cassettes hand over fist. . . ."

Asked whether he thinks women are aggressive DePalma responds: "Sure. They're being affected by the same system [capitalism] that men have been. If you want to change all of society you have to protest porn and General Motors simultaneously. I want to see WAP take that position."

Pally's interview is preceded by "Brian's Body," excerpts from the script of *Body Double,* 9–11.

Pasternak, Judith. "Censors in Feminist Clothing." *Savvy,* April
    1985, 14–15.
Pasternak delineates the potential negative results from censoring material. Says violence is depicted in so much media that it would make more sense "to investigate the root causes of that violence" rather than spend energy trying to eradicate pornography which is only one example of it.

Patterson, Wendy. "Sex Workers Oppose Pornography
    Legislation." *Womanews* (New York City), May 1985, 9.
Reports the author's view of the "MacKinnon-Hunter Debate" at the March 1985 Women In Law Conference in New York City. MacKinnon argued that "there must be ordinances allowing women to sue pornographers." Nan Hunter, an ACLU lawyer, argued that "this ordinance empowers the courts—not women—to decide legislation affecting our lives." Included is a brief mention that "women who work in the sex industry" fear the ordinance would threaten their livelihood.

Philipson, Ilene. "Beyond the Virgin and the Whore." *Socialist
    Review* 14, May–August 1984, 127–135.
Philipson says that many socialist-feminists are leaders of the attack on the feminist antipornography movement. She details the name calling on both sides and says both are too simplistic. Philipson says, "The antipornography movement and a number of socialist-feminists have resurrected the virgin and the whore. You have two alternatives: to be branded as a slut or taunted as a goody-goody." Philipson goes on to say, "Since the antipornography movement has been raked endlessly over the coals for being divisive,

exclusionary, and moralistic, I think it is time to examine its critics' role in the sexuality debate." She proceeds to do so.

Philipson, Ilene. "The Repression of History and Gender: A
    Critical Perspective on the Feminist Sexuality Debate." *Signs:
    Journal of Women in Culture and Society* 10, Autumn 1984,
    113–118.
    The author finds the case of prosex feminists unsatisfactory in its simplistic assumption that present society is sexually repressive and pornography liberating, and in its taking men as less-sexually repressed and therefore as sexual models. In their resistance to the antipornography position, this group of feminists has taken up an equally moralistic point of view.

Phillips, Michael, et al. "Violence in Pornography, or Not?"
    CoEvolution Quarterly 25, Spring 1980, 20–21.
    Report of a letter to Margo St. James, founder of COYOTE, the first prostitution union, by Michael Phillips who claims to have examined numerous porn shops and found no violence. This in response to St. James's denunciation of pornography.

Pilpel, Harriet F. "Porn Vigilantes—Are They Confusing Feminism
    With Censorship?" *Vogue,* September 1985, 681, 750.
    Pilpel is strongly opposed to the MacKinnon-Dworkin ordinance because she sees it as a form of censorship that violates constitutionally guaranteed freedom of speech and the press. She explains the status of the Indianapolis ordinance, quoting from the opinion of Judge Sarah Evans Barker and notes the other cities that have considered or attempted to pass similar ordinances. In summarizing her position she writes of freedom of speech and press: "It means freedom of expression for the ideas we hate."

"The Place of Pornography." *Harper's,* November 1984, 31–45.
    Report of a forum sponsored by *Harper's* at the New School for Social Research in New York City. Questions considered were: In a supposedly liberated society, what is the place of pornography? Why is it often grim and violent? And what, if anything, should we do about it? Participants were civil libertarians, feminists, social critics,

and a pornographer: Al Goldstein, Midge Decter, Erica Jong, Susan Brownmiller, Jean Bethke Elshtain, and Aryeh Neier.

"The Playboy Forum." *Playboy,* August 1986, 41–44.

The subtitle describes this feature as a "continuing dialog on contemporary issues between *Playboy* and its readers." Included are commentaries on the banning of the magazine by 7-Eleven stores; the attacks on *Ms* magazine by Women Against Pornography, for publishing a Calvin Klein ad; and letters written by John Updike, William Kennedy, Susan Isaacs, and John Irving which were sent to the Meese Commission, letters which "offered their testimony on the effects of censorship."

"Playboy Viewpoint: The New Puritans." *Playboy,* November 1980, 20–21, 30.

The book *Take Back the Night* (see entry under "Books" section) will serve as the *Mein Kampf* of the "new totalitarianism" by such women as those represented by the likes of Women Against Pornography. The author states that "for twenty-seven years, *Playboy* has tried to portray a healthful, robust sexuality based on equality of partners. . . . Now we find that the name-calling still exists—in the minds of Women Against Pornography."

"Porn." *Off Our Backs,* April 1983, 4, 5.

Reports on various happenings in the antipornography movement. There is an article on feminists in British Columbia campaigning against the Red Hot video stores, a chain selling pornographic video cassettes, which culminated in firebombings, jailing of some of the women, and strong statements of support from other Canadian feminist groups. Another report describes actions against sex shops in Britain and legal and other efforts to curtail them.

"A Porn Ban Fails in Maine." *Newsweek,* 23 June 1986, 33.

An account of the Maine obscenity referendum that was defeated by a two to one vote. A spokesman for the Christian Civic League, that supported the measure, "contended that feminists who are often antiporn and 'should have been our natural allies in this,' hold a grudge against his group because of its work in defeating the equal rights amendment in Maine two years ago." The referendum was opposed by the Maine Citizens Against Government Censorship, "an organization of feminists, lawyers, writers, teachers and librarians."

"Porn Commission Attacked and Defended at IFRT Program."
    American Libraries. July–August 1986, 524.
    Supporters and critics of the Attorney General's Commission on Pornography appeared on a program panel sponsored by the Intellectual Freedom Round Table of the American Library Association. Alan Sears, executive director of the commission, described procedures and summed up recommendations. Evelina Kane represented Women Against Pornography. Feminist Anti-Censorship Task Force member Marcia Pally gave her views that the belief that pornography causes violence against women is unproven, "a distraction that turns our attention away from the real causes of harm." Judy Blume also spoke.

"The Porno Plague." *Time,* 5 April 1976, 58–63.
    A cover story on pornography. The writers find "America is deep into its Age of Porn." Sketches the history of pornography in this country and the Supreme Court's rulings on it. Law enforcement action against pornography in New York City, San Francisco, Atlanta, and Boston is described. The article also considers the increase of sadomasochism in pornography and the movie *Snuff.* "Says Feminist Author Susan Brownmiller, who considers *Snuff* and all pornography strongly anti-female: 'If the porno houses were devoted to the lynching of blacks or the gassing of Jews, you would not find so many civil libertarians rushing to their defense.'" A special insert traces the growth of adult entertainment in Mason City, Iowa, from the mid-sixties to the present.

"Pornography: A Humanist Issue." *The Humanist* 45, July–August 1985, 23–31, 45.
    This is the transcript of a panel discussion on pornography sponsored by the Feminist Caucus of the American Humanist Association. Lester Kirkendall, the first speaker, feels the real issues are "learning how to educate ourselves about sexuality, learning how to educate ourselves about dealing with interpersonal relations which will be minus the violence which is too often found there."

Annie Laurie Gaylor feels pornography does great harm to women. She spoke in support of the Minneapolis ordinance: "There has to be a legal acknowledgment of the status of women who are harmed by pornography." Sol Gordon sees pornography as a symptom, rather than a cause of anything. He feels the need is for better sex education. He believes the Minneapolis ordinance is "an outrageous violation of civil liberties," and sees the whole issue as "a diversionary issue! It is destroying and limiting the humanist movement, the feminist movement." Gina Allen supports the Minneapolis ordinance, but has reservations about the support of the Moral Majority and Schlafly's Eagle Forum. "But Phyllis Schlafly wants to take away women's rights to their own bodies the minute they hit home."

The panelists also respond to several questions from the audience.

"Pornography: Love or Death? Twelve Vital Voices on the Eighties' Sexiest Debate." *Film Comment* 20, November–December 1984, 29–49.

Continuing a discussion begun, in an interview with Brian DePalma, in the previous issue of *Film Comment,* the editors asked twelve "experts in film, politics and the law" to address the question of images of sexual violence in films.

Responding were David Denby, film critic for *New York Magazine,* who finds the assumptions behind the MacKinnon-Dworkin ordinance, an "odd mixture of paranoia, illogic, and sheer obsession. . . ." Harvard Law School professor, Alan M. Dershowitz, writes about the "Faustian pact" the antipornography feminists have made with Rev. Jerry Falwell. Edward Donnerstein and Daniel Linz write about their research on sexually violent films and sexual aggression, as do Neil M. Malamuth and Jan Lindstrom. Margo St. James, founder of COYOTE, writes that "Good Girl feminists fail to connect the repeal of the prohibition on prostitution to emancipation." FACT member, Ann Snitow charges that the feminist antipornography measures "propose a moralism, an absolute boundary for expression, a sense of disgust or horror about the sexually explicit. It's all too hideously familiar."

Also responding are Al Goldstein, publisher of *Screw,* feminist Dorchen Leidholdt, attorney Janella Miller, writer Marcia Pally, Dr. Thomas Radecha, chairman of the National Coalition on Television

Violence, and Lois P. Sheinfeld, an attorney and associate professor of journalism and mass communication at New York University.

"Pornography: Obscene Profits at the Expense of Women." *Dollars & Sense* 39, September 1978, 12–14.

A survey of the growth of the pornography industry—both financially and in terms of the extremes of its content. One theory on the content of pornography is that it has gone to extremes because what was previously shocking is now common on television and in the movies. Another theory is that it is "part of a backlash against the women's movement." Larry Flynt agrees with this theory: "I'm in favor of the women's movement. It's just that they take no responsibility for scaring men. . . ." Feminist activities against pornography are briefly surveyed.

Posner, Judith. "Advertising Pornography." *The Canadian Forum*, August–September 1983, 12–16.

The author says there is "an increase of highly provocative and violent imagery in advertising" which indicates that "pornography as we once knew it has been co-opted by the establishment"—so porn itself has become "increasingly bizarre and perverse. . . ." A number of examples, including illustrations, are provided. Posner believes that the "current spate of violent pornography is the logical consequence" of male-female status differences.

Press, Aric, with Ann McDaniel. "Hard-Core Proposals." *Newsweek*, 28 April 1986, 38–39.

Report on the release of the tentative recommendations of the Meese Commission calling for "more criminal prosecutions, sterner regulation of cable television and the organizing of citizen groups to monitor what local bookstores sell over the counter." Notes the division among the commissioners with "many votes reportedly divided six to five." Goes on to report the commission may already be having an impact as evidenced by the 7-Eleven chain's decision to no longer sell *Penthouse* and *Playboy*.

Preston, John. "Gay Men and Feminists Have Reached a Fork in the Road." *Christopher Street* 5, 1981, 17–26.

Details the issue of pornography as seen by women and by gay men. He describes the dichotomy thus: "To women the experience and fear of unleashed male sexuality in the form of rape is the most naked expression of women's domination by men. Freedom from rape is the first, necessary step toward women's liberation. Anything that glorifies, encourages, or forgives rape—actually or symbolically—is intolerable. To women, pornography is precisely such a symbolic act of rape. To gay men the fear of one's own sexuality . . . is the most pernicious expression of sexism in our society. . . . The acceptance of our bodies, the unhindered celebration of our sexuality, and the act of loving each other. Anything that helps to free our repressed selves—including pornography—has a positive value." Preston details how the women's movement and gay men's liberation movement have come apart, and differences over pornography constitute one of the major issues. "Feminists insist on perceiving adult bookstores as pandering to the most sexist, base, dangerous men." In fact, "adult bookstores in small-city America," says Preston, "are the only conduits for national gay media."

"Rampage Against Penthouse Magazine . . ." *Womanews* (New York City), May 1985, 4.
    The rampage against *Penthouse* magazine, staged by Nikki Craft and the Preying Mantis Women's Brigade, has now converged on fourteen communities in different parts of the country. Over forty-eight people have destroyed hundreds of *Penthouse* magazines in fifty-five bookstores, newsstands, pornshops, and convenience stores in six states, resulting in many arrests. The action was being done "in retaliation for the December 1984 issue of *Penthouse* which showed Japanese women tied up, hung from trees and hurled onto rocks, several appearing to be dead."

"The Red Hot Debate, Continued." *The Body Politic,* September 1983, 4–6.
    A collection of letters dealing with pornography and violence against women, especially centering around an ad in the June 1983 issue of *The Body Politic* for the "Red Hot Video."

Rich, Adrienne. "We Don't Have to Come Apart Over Pornography." *Off Our Backs,* July 1985, 30, 32.
    Rich tells why she signed the FACT *amicus curiae* brief on the Indianapolis antipornography ordinance. She saw the brief as a flawed but important attempt to consider such legislation within the

context of a generally violent, increasingly repressive, antifeminist, racist . . . society. Rich says she does not like pornography but does not believe that pornography is "central in creating and maintaining the civil inequality of the sexes." Rich says further, "I am more and more loathe to ascribe to any one cause the subordination of women, the prevalence of male violence. . . ." She goes on to describe more of her beliefs about this and related issues.

Ridington, Jillian. "Pornography: What Does the New Research
     Say?" *Status of Women News/La Revue de L'Etate de la Femme* 8,
     Summer 1983.
     Reviews various research reports from scientists, feminists, and others. Notes the confusion of pornography with erotica. Describes briefly relevant Canadian laws, "made by the federal government," but "responsibility for implementing them lies with the provinces. Attitudes and procedures towards enforcement vary among provinces."

Rollins, Chiquita. "When Conservatives Investigate Porn . . ." *Off
     Our Backs,* December 1985, 1, 12–13.
     Report of the first of six public hearings held by the U.S. Attorney General's Commission on Pornography. The charge of the commission is to "determine the nature, extent and impact on society of pornography . . . and to make specific recommendations of ways in which the spread of pornography could be contained . . . consistent with constitutional guarantees." During the two days of these first hearings in Washington, approximately forty persons testified, among them D.C. Feminists Against Pornography and Women Against Pornography. Attorney General Edwin Meese III appointed the commission of eleven members. "Most of them seem predisposed against pornography. . . . One of their main objectives appeared to be to determine whether pornography causes violence against women." Rollins discusses the probable reasons for the appointment of a commission at this time.

Rossi, Lee D. "The Whore vs. the Girl-Next-Door: Stereotypes of
     Women in *Playboy, Penthouse,* and *Oui.*" *Journal of Popular
     Culture* 9, Summer 1975, 90–94.
     Points out that the so-called soft-core pornographic magazines support open sexuality, said to be one of the aims of women's

liberation, but reject social and economic equality with men. The article contrasts the "well-scrubbed sexuality" of *Playboy* with the "decadent sexuality" of *Penthouse* and *Oui*. All three magazines are said to be demeaning and repugnant to the women's movement.

Rubenstein, David. "Pornography Law Splits Minneapolis." *In These Times,* 18–24 January 1984, 1, 6.

The author provides the background for how the proposed ordinance, by MacKinnon and Dworkin, came about. A previous ordinance is described as are demonstrations, speeches, the civil right background of Minneapolis, and the controversy evoked between the civil libertarian and the antipornography proponent.

Russ, Joanna. "Pornography and the Doubleness of Sex for Women." *13th Moon* 8, 1984, 19–29.

Concerned with the bitterness within the women's movement over pornography and the fight against it, the author believes that a possible explanation may be the "doubleness of sexual experience— women whose sexual education has been horrendous (for example, those who have been raped repeatedly by an adult male relative) also have to deal with some positive feeling. . . ." Even women whose experiences have been more positive "cannot entirely escape this culture's negatives." She considers how these differences and this "doubleness" may influence one's position in the antipornography debate.

Russell, Diana E. H. "On Pornography." *Chrysalis,* 1, c.1977, 11–15.

Russell says most women have not dealt with pornography because it's too difficult to confront such women hatred. She calls pornography vicious, antiwoman propaganda and blames the report of the National Commission on Obscenity and Pornography, its findings determined by a male bias, for the proliferation of pornography since its release in 1970. Russell also says "the First Amendment was never intended to protect material that condones and promotes violence against any group."

Sanford, Linda Tschirhart, and Mary Ellen Donovan. "You Can
 Stop Pornography." *Reader's Digest,* June 1982, 181–183,
 185–186.
 The authors survey the growth in the pornography business and
the change in its content to include children and "violence, degradation and humiliation rather than plain sex." They briefly explain the
"catharsis, or release, theory" about the effects of pornography and
the "imitation theory." They believe pornography is harmful to both
women and men, and to sex itself. To combat it they list several
organizations to contact, including Women Against Pornography,
and suggest boycotts of supermarkets and drugstores that sell pornography, among other strategies recommended.
 Condensed from *Family Circle.*

Scheer, Robert. "Inside the Meese Commission." *Playboy,* August
 1986, 157–167.
 Scheer reports on his interview of Henry E. Hudson, chair of
the U.S. Attorney General's Commission on Pornography. This
"investigative report" describes Hudson's past antipornography activities, his working definition of pornography, and the commission's record of activities. Scheer provides biographical data on
commission members and describes his disagreement with Hudson.
The author traveled to all the hearings and notes "the feminist
connection." He reports the commission's lack of budget for research
and independent study. Scheer provides his analysis of the commission, "what is ugly and what is acceptable."

Scheinmann, Vivian J. "Speaking Personally." *New Directions for
 Women,* January–February 1985, 2.
 Scheinmann, a feminist bookseller, discusses the dilemma she
finds herself in with regard to the MacKinnon-Dworkin antipornography ordinance. "What is likely is that 1984 was only the
beginning of what will turn out to be a long on-going process of
what it means when some feminists attempt to influence legislators
across the country in passing laws that will affect what other
feminists choose to publish, distribute, sell, and display for consumption by yet another group of feminists."

Schipper, Henry. "Filthy Lucre." *Mother Jones* April 1980, 31–33, 60–62.

This article is a description of "a tour of America's most profitable frontier" the "adult entertainment center." The author details his visit to Show World in New York's Times Square. He gives figures on the profits in this and adult bookstores. He interviewed a man who produces live sex shows who, when asked "You don't think you degrade women for profit?" responded "I know I do." He also interviewed a woman who worked in such a show. She earns $130.00 a week. He visits a sex shop and interviews a porn filmmaker. In each and every case, he attaches the price tags.

"Sex and Violence Revisited." *Journal of Communication* 34, Summer 1984, 100–173.

This issue of the journal features articles on research on violence against women. "New empirical studies and cultural analysis extend and challenge theories about the deterrent effects of publicized executions; violent pornography, rape, and desensitization; and the political uses of media effects research." Three of the research reports deal with violence and pornography.

Shea, Robert. "Women at War (Against Pornography)." *Playboy*, February 1980, 86, 88, 90, 92, 179, 182, 184, 185.

Shea chronicles activities of Women against Pornography and other feminist attacks on porn in the United States and in other countries. He says "this feminist crusade is not aimed at hardcore pornography alone but against any sexy material that arouses its ire. . . ." He delineates what "they say" (the feminists) and his criticism of their beliefs and opinions. He also quotes the feminists who see positive values in pornography. Shea describes previous attempts to censor materials. He worries that the antipornography movement lures women away from more important issues and "plays into the hands of those who do not want to see women make real progress." He concludes that an end to pornography would do nothing to end crime against women.

Sheinfeld, Lois P. "Anti-Obscenity Ordinances: Banning Porn: The New Censorship." *The Nation*, 8 September 1984, 174–175.

Review of the activities and issues in the antipornography movement: the ordinances proposed in Minneapolis and Indianapolis, the First Amendment issues, the issues of violence, and the influence on behavior. Ms. Sheinfeld, an attorney, says that because there is an absence of an unchallengeable connection between pornography and sexual aggression, "It is therefore not surprising that the new antipornography ordinances abandon reliance on the serious-harm exception to the First Amendment and instead categorically declare pornography a violation of women's civil rights."

Silbert, Mimi H., and Ayala M. Pinas. "Pornography and Sexual Abuse of Women." *Sex Roles* 10, June 1984, 857–868.
Reports previous studies on the link between pornography and violence: 1970 report of the Commission on Obscenity and Pornography which concluded there was no connection, the Kronhausen's safety valve theory, the Danish experience, a study by Savity and Johnson on prisoners, and several others. On the other hand, the authors report on the growing body of literature "supporting an 'imitation model' of pornography." The article then covers the authors' research which they state makes it "clear that there is a relationship between violent pornography and sexual abuse in the experience of street prostitutes." Current and former female prostitutes in the San Francisco area reported their experiences of sexual assault in a questionnaire that contained items related to family and personal background, assault experiences, sexual exploitation as juveniles, self-concept, and future plans. Content analysis of the responses, showing numerous reports of rape by seventy-three percent and of juvenile abuse (by sixty percent), revealed that in almost twenty-five percent of these instances the abuser had made references to pornographic films, literature, or other material. A large group (thirty-eight percent) also said that they had been subjects in sexual photographs as children. "The data support the large body of research claiming that pornography serves as an 'imitation model' for sexual abuse."

Small, Fred. "Pornography and Censorship." *Changing Men* 15, Fall 1985, 7–8, 43–45.
Small acknowledges that as a man, he is not hurt and enraged by pornography in the same way as women, and that some will believe as a consequence, he has nothing to contribute. However, he is concerned about the dangers of censorship. He strongly opposes censorship because it can be used to suppress efforts for radical

change. Further, he says that he denounces pornography along with "all sexist propaganda. But I suspect that pornography is not the central problem of patriarchy, that it is more symptom than disease. . . . Pornography may not be the best target for our rage." The article develops further his beliefs, analysis of the dangers and inappropriateness of the antipornography movement, and proposes other alternatives.

Smith, Marjorie M. "Violent Pornography and the Women's
   Movement." *The Civil Liberties Review,* January–February
   1978, 50–53.
   Reports on campaigns against "sex violence" in media by Women Against Violence Against Women in Los Angeles. Says support for this type of activity is spreading. The author, at the time an ACLU lawyer, examines these actions and their impact on First Amendment rights.

Stanton, Therese. "Fighting for Our Existence." *Changing Men* 15,
   Fall 1985, 21–23.
   Stanton supports the use of civil rights ordinances. She believes they provide for women, as victims of violence, the opportunity "to plunge into the factual world—the sphere of existence. Being granted legal existence might make it possible for her to get the gag out of her mouth and to speak to all those men looking at her image."

Steinem, Gloria. "Erotica and Pornography: A Clear and Present
   Difference." *Ms,* November 1978, 53.
   One of the issues most frequently raised in debate about pornography and what to do about it involves separating it from erotica, which is considered positive. Steinem provides insights on how to distinguish between the two.

Steinem, Gloria. "Not Sex But the Obscene Use of Power." *Ms,*
   August 1977, 43–44.
   A discussion of the ways in which one can distinguish between erotica and pornography. One point made is the root of definition: "Erotica is rooted in 'eros' or passionate love, and thus is the idea of positive choice, free will . . . 'pornography' begins with a root 'porn,'

meaning 'prostitution' or 'female captives.' " She offers suggestions for learning to tell the difference.

Stengel, Richard. "Sex Busters." *Time*, 21 July 1986, 12–18,
    21–22.
An essay on the Meese Commission and its final report. Stengel gives a summary of how the commission operated and its final recommendations. The cover story also considers the commission in the broader context of shift in prevailing morals. "It [the commission] serves to document the evolving attitudes toward sexual morality that have gained acceptance during the Reagan era." The recent Supreme Court decision on sodomy, and the political power of the New Right are also discussed.

"Still on the Rampage Against *Penthouse*." *Off Our Backs*, January
    1986, 19.
Report of actions by Citizens for Media Responsibility Without Law against *Penthouse*. "With 108 arrests to their credit," there is no sign of slowing down their "Rampage Against *Penthouse*" organized by Nikki Craft. This article reports on a series of actions which took place in Durham, North Carolina. Other actions in Madison, Wisconsin and plans for Missouri and Pennsylvania are mentioned. The rampage has been directed at many B. Dalton bookstores which sell *Penthouse*. The boycott of *Penthouse* advertisers is beginning to work, according to this report.

Tong, Rosemarie. "Feminism, Pornography and Censorship." *Social
    Theory and Practice*, 8, Spring 1982, 1–17.
This paper argues that a certain kind of pornography is degrading to women, that it is possible to distinguish this type of pornography from other types, and that "Constitutional principles, somewhat different than those stressed in the Supreme Court's leading obscenity decisions, warrant the imposition of legal constraints on publicly disseminated, degrading pornographic material."

Tong, Rosemarie. "The Minneapolis Ordinance and the FACT
    Brief." *The Women's Review of Books*, 3 May 1986, 7–9.
Tong provides the legal history of the antipornography ordinance first tested in Minneapolis in 1982 and states why feminist

antipornographers have "eschewed both the 'obscenity' approach and the 'zoning' approach to pornography." The feminist antipornographers are interested in "women's political equality and not women's moral conformity—especially conformity to a moral ideal that has contributed and probably still is contributing to our subordination." The zoning laws view pornography as merely a distressing nuisance whereas the antipornographers see it as dangerous to women and also as elitist. Tong details the criticism of Feminists Against Pornography and others regarding the ordinance. Tong closes her piece with suggestions for further address of the problems of pornography.

"TRB From Washington: Reagan's Pornographer." *New Republic,*
    30 June 1986, 4.
The writer finds it curious that the U.S. Attorney General's Commission on Pornography finds a causal link between pornography and violence, while President Reagan on the other hand invites Sylvester Stallone, star of the movie *Cobra* which "directly advocates violence, glamorizes its practitioners," to the White House. "But I marvel at the cognitive dissonance that allows the Reagan administration to explore uncharted passages around the First Amendment in search of ways to stifle *Playboy* and *Penthouse*—ostensible because of some connection to encouraging violence—while outright embracing Sylvester Stallone."

Turley, Donna. "The Feminist Debate on Pornography." *Socialist
    Review* 16, May–August 1986, 81–94.
Turley says that women's first efforts to focus on the image of women's sexuality as depicted by male culture were directed at all media, at stores, at advertising, at products and took the form of Take Back the Night marches, boycotts of stores and products, writing, lecturing, and classroom teaching. Some women in the movement chose to focus on pornography. The author claims this happened because of the rise of the new right and the election of Ronald Reagan: women suffered many losses and "pornography was an easy choice [among issues] since it is one of the most blatant examples of misogyny available." Turley describes the "History of the [Dworkin and MacKinnon] ordinance," analyzes its contents, and details the feminist objections to it. She concludes with recommen-

dations for going "Beyond Pornography" to deal with the exploitation of women.

"Two Commissioners Demand More Data." *New Directions for Women,* July–August 1986, 6.

Two members of the Meese Commission on Pornography, Judith Becker and Ellen Levine, state the "limitations" and "constraints" around the work of the commission. They believe that more work is needed on the subject of pornography, and that core issues around pornography should best be considered by the National Institute of Mental Health, not law enforcement agencies and Attorney General Meese.

Tysoe, Maryon. "The Porno Effect." *New Society* 71, 7 March 1985, 358.

A survey of the research studies done by Edward Donnerstein at the University of Wisconsin and Neil Malamuth at the University of Manitoba on the effects of violent pornography on behavior. Tysoe summarizes: "Utterly conclusive research in this kind of area is very hard to obtain." She concludes, "Perhaps we should concentrate more on the way attitudes to women, sex, and violence are shaped in our society that so many men lap up the stuff in the first place."

Vance, Carol S., and Ann Barr Snitow. "Toward a Conversation About Sex in Feminism: A Modest Proposal." *Signs: Journal of Women in Culture and Society* 10, Autumn 1984, 126–134.

The authors say that it is difficult to assess the recent debates about sexuality within American feminism because "we inherit an inadequate vocabulary to describe women's experience." The debates, they say, were followed by the relatively unchallenged antipornography organizing and theorizing, and this was then followed by reaction and counterreaction. The authors proceed with an analysis of various factions, and their views of sexual behavior and what conditions it, and the errors of the antipornography movement.

Van Gelder, Lindsy. "Playboy's Charity: Is It Reparations or Rip-Off?" *Ms,* June 1983, 78.

Discusses the dilemma over accepting money from an organization that many believe contributes to abuse of women. Poses questions as to whether the Playboy Foundation is more harmful to women than the federal government. Notes that several people— Donna Shalala, Charles Nesson, Gene Reynolds—resigned from the panel of judges for the Hugh M. Hefner First Amendment Awards under pressure from antipornography groups.

Van Gelder, Lindsy. "Pornography Goes to Washington." *Ms,* June 1986, 52–54, 83.
Van Gelder attended the Meese Commission hearings held in New York which "officially dealt with the relationship between pornography and organized crime." She describes the testimony of various law enforcement officials and several representatives of religious organizations. The most audience hostility, however, was directed at Andrea Dworkin. Because Dworkin and the anticensorship group share a common past ". . . she's seen by the anticensorship side as not just an adversary, but a turncoat. . . . The bottom line is that Dworkin is seen as threatening in a way that the far more powerful true-believing vice cops and religious nuts aren't." Also testifying were Linda Marciano and former *Penthouse* centerfold, Dottie Meyer. "More than anything else, these two presentations told me how the issue is defined outside the feminist cocoon—and the issue is not whether pornography destroys or exalts the souls of women, but whether or not it interferes with the carrying out of traditional female roles."

Van Gelder, Lindsy. "When Women Confront Street Porn." *Ms,* February 1980, 62–66, 89.
Description of the Women Against Pornography slide show and of their "twice-weekly guided tours of the Times Square (New York City) neighborhood's live sex shows, peep shows, dirty bookstores, and topless bars." Some views of interviews of the male patrons. She dates the current wave of feminist action against violent porn as beginning in 1976 when "an ad hoc New York group picketed the movie *Snuff.*"

"Violent Pornography: Degradation of Women Versus Right of Free Speech." *New York University Review of Law and Social Change* 8, 1978–1979, 181–300.
A colloquium featuring speeches, debates, a slide show, panel and audience discussions on the various issues and confrontations

between antipornography activists and defenders of the First Amendment. Among those participating and recorded here are Andrea Dworkin, Leah Fritz, Phyllis Chesler, Paul Chevegny, David Richards, and many others. As with most articles in law journals, there are numerous references in the footnotes.

Vloebersk, Assomption. "Does Pornography Incite Violence?" *La Recherche*, June 1979, 682–684.
    A discussion of the relationship between pornography and violence, particularly toward women, with emphasis on a recent study by Donnerstein and Hallam (*Journal of Personality and Social Psychology*, November 1978, 1270–1277) that examined, through a series of complex manipulations, the relationship between viewing a pornographic film and later administering electric shocks to another subject—who was actually an experimenter. While findings seem to indicate some relationship between the two, it would be premature to conclude that pornography is responsible for aggression against women. Further, the methods used in the experiment are called into question.

Wagner, Sally Roesch. "Suffrage in the 1870's and Anti-Pornography in the 1980's." *Changing Men* 15, Fall 1985, 26–27.
    The author posits an analogy between the radical feminist suffrage work in the 1870s, "that particular historical moment when the denial of voting rights to women emerged as a primary cultural contradiction, and when a particular group of radical feminists struggled bravely and intensely to heighten that contradiction as a means of gaining liberation for all women . . ." and the current antipornography movement. In our particular historical moment, "pornography similarly emerges as a primary cultural contradiction, heightened by a particular group of radical feminists as a means of gaining liberation for all women." The article provides evidence for the contradiction in society and further support for the validity of the analogy.

Walby, Sylvia, Alex Hay, and Keith Soothill. "The Social Construction of Rape." *Theory, Culture and Society* 2, 1983, 86–98.
    One element in the discourse on rape is systematically analyzed—the reporting of rape events in newspapers. The frequency of

twenty-one elements of rape images in a sample of six newspapers in one year was examined, contrasting these images with evidence collected by social scientists from official crime statistics, police records, and population surveys. The dominant image of rape in newspapers was of acts committed by men, permanently or temporarily out of control, against women, who provoked the attack by their sexual conduct or the place in which they put themselves. These images were not borne out by the other sources of evidence. It is argued that newspaper reports misleadingly sexualize rape, frequently presenting it as a form of soft pornography in order to boost declining sales.

"War Against Pornography: Feminists, Free Speech and the Law." *Newsweek,* 18 March 1985, 58–67.

Cover story report on the "unusual coalition of feminists and fundamentalists" who believe that violence in pornography encourages violence against women. It reports results of a Gallup poll which showed that nearly two-thirds of those surveyed supported a ban on magazines, movies, and videos that feature sexual violence. A general survey of the issues, the proposals, and the battles.

"We, the Wimmin's Fire Brigade, Claim Responsibility." *Heresies, A Feminists Publication on Art and Politics* 4, Issue 16, 1983, 17.

Report, in the Film/Video issue of *Heresies,* of the fire bombing of three Red Hot Video outlets in British Columbia on 22 November 1982. The Brigade says, "This action is another step towards the destruction of a business that promotes and profits from violence against wimmin and children." The Brigade says that illegal means are necessary because although the tapes sold show women being tortured and raped, and violate the Criminal Code of Canada, nothing happens to stop the sale because the justice system is created and controlled by rich men.

Webster, Paula. "Pornography and Pleasure." *Heresies: A Feminist Publication on Art and Politics* 3, Issue 12, 1981, 48–51.

This records an experience of a slide show of pornography and a tour of Forty-second Street and the "need for discussion of our many contradictory reactions to what had been seen." She says there was no discussion because the lines between good sex and bad sex had been drawn. Webster believes feminists should concentrate on an analysis of female sexuality, not men and violence, and create a pornography of their own.

Weir, Lorna and Leo Casey. "Subverting Power in Sexuality." *Socialist Review* 14, May–August 1984,139–157.
The authors say that the relationship between power and sexuality raises a variety of difficult questions for socialists attempting to develop a progressive sexual politics. The women's and gay movements insist that there is a vital interconnection between power and sexuality but there is no agreement how this is to be understood. The authors outline some present theories and criticize their shortcomings. They give recommendations for a better foundation for political strategy using the two major camps in the focus on pornography as a basis for theoretical development.

Weiss, Philip. "Forbidden Pleasures: A Taste for Porn in a City of Women." *Harper's* 272, March 1986, 68–72.
Weiss, a reporter in Minneapolis when that city was debating the MacKinnon-Dworkin antipornography bill, writes about his reactions as a man and casual consumer of pornography to the bill. "For a year the antiporn movement seemed to be the strongest voice in the city, and I now see that shame, the manipulation of traditional pruderies, was an important factor in its success." In retrospect Weiss believes the proper response would be that proposed by Tim Campbell in *GLC Voice,* a gay newspaper: "I believe that men are going to have to do more than avoid the issues of content of pornography to satisfactorily deal with the 'radical feminists.' Men are going to have to stand up and own their use of pornography. They are going to have to explain what goes on with them as they view pornography."

"What Sort of Woman Hates *Playboy?*" *Playboy,* February 1980, 181.
Interview of "militant feminist," Marcia Womongold, by television interviewer, Joe Oteri. Womongold presents the view that pornography is antiwoman and prompts violence. Womongold believes women should defend themselves. Oteri worries about vigilantes.

Whisman, Vera. "Lesbianism, Feminism, and Social Science."
Humanity and Society 8, November 1984, 453–460.

Lesbianism's redefinition as a primarily political, rather than sexual, stance is a source of disagreement among feminists; it is criticized for being ahistorical, displaying an antisex bias, being elitist, and alienating feminist women from each other. Definitions of pornography are another source of conflict among feminists. With reference to the sociology of deviance and labeling theory, it is argued that the true conflict involves larger sociological issues revolving around causal explanation and interpretation; problems of feminist theory are problems of social theory in general.

White, Van F. "Pornography and Pride." *Changing Men* 15, Fall 1985, 17–18.

White reports how his feelings have changed about pornography, especially since "being the first person of color ever elected to the city council of Minneapolis." He says of pornography stores, "They always seem to be put in the poorest of the communities— where black, Native American, Hispanic, and poor whites are living. But in the finer parts of the city you don't find them. . . ." He recounts his experiences of conducting public hearings on pornography. He is a cosponsor of the Minneapolis civil rights, pornography ordinance.

Wildwomoon, Shell. "We Will Not Be Silent Victims." *WIN*, 1 December 1980, 16–20.

Details of some examples of women's illegal and legal resistance to pornography, especially an attack on a porn shop in Hartford, Connecticut and the resulting arrest and trial. The author and her two colleagues are "committed to nonviolent actions against all forms of violence against life." "We would not use legal means for fighting back . . ." because laws are used against women.

"Women Against Pornography Picks '84 Best/Worst Ads." *Southern Feminist*, May–June 1985, 17.

Report of the Fourth Annual Advertising Awards ceremony at the Women Against Pornography headquarters in New York City. Five American advertisers were honored for their ads which portrayed "women as they are and as they wish to be seen." Six other advertisers were criticized for "ads which use the tenets of pornography to sell their products."

"Women's War on Porn: Feminists Organize Against Smut." *Time*, 27 August 1979, 64.

A news report of feminist groups throughout the country taking to the streets to demonstrate their feelings about pornography—and the reactions and reasons of those who oppose them.

Zawinski, Andrena. "Pornography is Violence Against Women." *Off Our Backs*, July 1980, 8–9.

Report of the Conference on Pornography: A Feminist Perspective at the University of Pittsburgh, May 1980. Researchers Donnerstein and Malamuth joined Florence Rush and other New York, Chicago, and Pittsburgh feminists to examine pornography as an issue of violence against women. There were workshops on lesbians and pornography, on how to distinguish erotica from pornography, on the nature of pornography as it relates to woman-battering, and on sexism in pornography. First Amendment absolutists, right-wing and radical-feminist philosophies were discussed at the conference.

Zillman, Dolf, and Jennings Bryant. "Pornography, Sexual Callousness, and the Trivialization of Rape." *Journal of Communication* 32, Autumn 1982, 10–21.

A report of research that indicates that "under controlled experimental conditions, massive exposure to pornography resulted in a loss of compassion toward women as rape victims and toward women in general." Quotes many feminists leaders of the antipornography movement.

3.
Newspapers

The major newspapers included in this bibliography are the *New York Times, Washington Post, Christian Science Monitor,* and *Los Angeles Times.* These papers were thought to have the greatest availability, in microfilm format, to the greatest number of readers. Special interest newspapers such as the *Village Voice* and *Gay Community News* are included because of the relevance and frequency of articles on the antipornography topic. Articles from the *Boston Globe* for 1985 are given for their coverage of the Cambridge antipornography referendum in the November 1985 election.

For a chronological approach to this material, see appendix B.

"ACLU Debates 'Rights in Conflict.' " *Civil Liberties,* Summer 1985.

The report of an American Civil Liberties Union conference in Boulder, Colorado in June. In one debate, Catharine MacKinnon denounced ACLU for its opposition to antipornography ordinances, "for supporting the 'pimps of pornography.' " ACLU general counsel Harriet Pilpel countered with criticism that MacKinnon and her followers were unable to "distinguish between action and speech."

Adams, Marianne. "Something for Everyone." *Village Voice,* 14 September 1982, 40.

A woman who describes herself as a worker in a "three-level sex emporium on Times Square" describes what she does and how she feels about it. She is very critical about the organization, Women Against Pornography.

Alexander, Priscilla. "Speaking Out: A Response to Andrea Dworkin." *Gay Community News,* 8 February 1986, 5.

Alexander, education coordinator for COYOTE, writes in response to an interview with Andrea Dworkin published in the 28 December–4 January issue of *Gay Community News.* She agrees with Dworkin that it is time to end violence against women as entertainment. "However, our agreement stops there. Dworkin supports legislation dealing with *content*. I don't. Instead, I support legislation dealing with the *action*, that is, the sexual assault itself, whether or not the work produced depicts sexual activity."

She charges Dworkin and MacKinnon "have internalized the patriarchial meaning of the word *whore*, and use the word to judge women as men have done." She is critical of their ordinance because, "it [the law] will be in the hands of judges, few of whom are women, fewer of whom are feminists, and juries from which thinking, progressive, aware people are routinely excluded." In addition, Alexander refutes Dworkin's criticisms of FACT. She also criticizes Dworkin for her dismissal of the First Amendment as being written by white males for white males.

Basler, Barbara. "5,000 Join Feminist Group's Rally in Times
    Square Against Pornography." *New York Times,* 21 October
    1979, sec. A, 41.
    Report on the demonstration against pornography, organized by Women Against Pornography, that drew 5,000 people. The protesters marched through Times Square and held a rally in Bryant Park. At the rally a WAP founder, Lynn Campbell, urged women "to go out into their communities and 'take action—form consciousness-raising and education campaigns against pornography.' "

Bennetts, Leslie. "Conference Examines Pornography As A
    Feminist Issue." *New York Times,* 17 September 1979,
    sec. B, 10.
    Bennetts reports on the East Coast feminist conference sponsored by Women Against Pornography, held in New York City on 15-16 September. Explaining why the women's movement is taking up this issue, Gloria Steinem said: "It's organic, in a way: having untangled sex and violence on the issue of rape, which came first because it's direct physical violence—as opposed to pornography which is indirect—then it's a rational progression toward untangling sex and violence in pornography." On the issue of First Amendment rights Bella Abzug said: "I do not believe it is necessary for us to interfere with anyone's constitutional right to produce pornography. But that doesn't require us to encourage and assist in the proliferation of pornographic materials on the streets and in the stores." The

conference, which was made up of lectures, workshops, panels, films and discussions, was attended by 700 women.

Blumenthal, Karen. "Adult-Magazine Ban Brings Cries of
    Censorship." *Wall Street Journal,* eastern ed., 14 April
    1986, 31.
    A report on the decision by Southland Corporation to stop selling *Playboy, Penthouse* and *Forum* in its 7-Eleven stores. Company officials "say that they also were influenced by testimony before a national pornography commission" in making this decision. Barry Lynn, of the ACLU, and William F. Gorog, president of the Magazine Publishers Association, are quoted opposing this action.
    See the *Journal* for 24 April, eastern ed., 31, for a letter in support of Southland Corporation written by Marie Caesar, a member of Feminists Fighting Pornography.

Buchwald, Art. "First Amendment's Passionate Protector." *Los
    Angeles Times,* 5 April 1984, sec. 5, 3.
    Buchwald is pleased that the Minneapolis mayor vetoed the antipornography ordinance because with such legislation "you run into the problem of where degradation stops and mind-boggling romance takes over." To prove his point he quotes from the recently published *The Romance Writers' Phrase Book* by Jean Kent and Candace Shelton (New York: Putnam Publishing Group, 1984).

Bush, Larry. "Blinding Us With Science: The Antiporn Activist as
    Reaganite." *Village Voice,* 20 March 1984, 19–20.
    An essay on the U.S. Justice Department's $800,000 grant to Dr. Judith Reisman for a 'biological/neurophysiological' study "in which the male response to pornography, and its effect on violent crime, can be clinically defined." Bush is critical of Reisman's credentials for such a project, pointing out inaccuracies regarding membership in professional organizations on her vita and the fact that she has not published "any serious work on pornography." He recounts her feminist background and the fact that "by the time her grant proposal reached the Reagan administration, Reisman's view of the importance of those issues had shifted." Also covered are grants to the University of Pennsylvania and the Rand Corporation on related

topics—"all aimed at linking biological factors to allegedly rising juvenile delinquency."

Byron, Peg. "The New Pro-Inhibition." *Village Voice,* 5 June
     1984, 46.
     Byron surveys recent legislation against pornography: the tougher child pornography law signed by Reagan the previous week, the announcement of the formation of a national Commission on Pornography, and the passage of the Indianapolis ordinance the previous month.

Byron, Peg. "Smutbusters!" *Village Voice,* 27 November 1984, 50.
     A news article on the fact that New York City Councilwoman, Miriam Friedlander, would like to see a MacKinnon-Dworkin type bill introduced in council and discussion of the repercussions of such legislation in New York City. Andrea Dworkin says she "doesn't want to pursue legislation here: 'I live in New York, and people have been ferocious.' "

Califia, Pat. "Among Us, Against Us—The New Puritans." *The
     Advocate,* 17 April 1980.
     Califia questions the equation of pornography with violence adding up to political repression. She says, "Only if one thinks of sex itself as a degrading act can one believe that all pornography degrades and harms women." She details her criticism of groups such as Women Against Violence in Pornography and the Media who "are threatening the sexual freedom rights of others." She says they are procensorship and antisex in their positions and that few members of the liberal press will risk opposing them.

Carelli, Richard. "Supreme Court Rejects Pornography
     Ordinance." *Boston Globe,* 25 February 1986, 3.
     A report on the Supreme Court decision that the Indianapolis antipornography ordinance "impermissably [*sic*] interferes with free speech." Gives the history of the ordinance and summaries of the lower court's decisions against it. "In Cambridge, Massachusetts, last fall, an ordinance patterned after the Indianapolis measure was rejected by voters after a campaign waged by a local group, Women Against Pornography."

"The Censors Among Us." *Los Angeles Times*. 28 February 1985, sec. 2, 4.

An editorial against the proposed antipornography ordinance before the Los Angeles Board of Supervisors. While sympathetic to those who oppose pornography the editors continue: "But prohibiting the publication or distribution of such material is far more dangerous than the material itself. The proponents of this measure should know better."

"Censors Fail to See the Danger." *Los Angeles Times*, 25 November 1984, sec. 4, 4.

Editorial in support of U.S. District Court Judge Sarah Barker's ruling against the Indianapolis antipornography ordinance. The writers note hearings are to begin next month in Los Angeles on a similar ordinance. "Supporters of the legislation should heed Barker's reasoning and not go down the path of censorship explored by Indianapolis."

"Censors in Feminist Garb." *New York Times*, 19 November 1984, sec. A, 22.

An editorial strongly against the antipornography bill before the Suffolk County, New York legislature, similar to those proposed in Minneapolis, Indianapolis, and Los Angeles. The editors see no substance in the claim that pornography is a violation of women's civil rights, and great danger in the fact that such legislation "would all too easily permit a further ban on any kind of expression, sexual or not, that offends anyone."

"Censors in White Robes." *Los Angeles Times*, 3 August 1984, sec. 3, 4.

Editorial on the Indianapolis antipornography ordinance federal court case. The writers believe this ordinance ". . . may be the most dangerous threat to free speech in this country in many years because the law comes clothed in the appealing white robes of antipornography." To an ordinance supporter's claim that the First Amendment involves a balancing with other interests the writers reply, "That specious theory is always argued to drape the censor in a cloak of respectability. . . ."

"Censorship and Pornography." *Los Angeles Times,* 10 September
    1984, sec. 2, 4.

Editorial critical of Los Angeles City Councilman, Ernani
Bernardi, and his Public Health, Human Resources, and Senior
Citizens Committee for considering an antipornography ordinance
patterned after Indianapolis. ". . . the Indianapolis ordinance represents the very essence of censorship that cannot be tolerated under
the First Amendment." The writers are also critical of San Diego
City Councilwoman, Gloria McColl, for proposing "a state law that
would award $50,000 to a person whose civil rights are violated by
pornography."

"Censorship Is No One's Civil Right." *New York Times,* 27 May
    1984, sec. D, 16.

Editorial against the Indianapolis City Council antipornography ordinance, describing it as an "end run around the First
Amendment." While agreeing with Women Against Pornography
and other groups that smut is degrading—both to women and
men—it says, "But the American way to combat one kind of speech
is with other speech, and through legal economic pressure."

For two letters to the editor disagreeing with this editorial see
"A Shield Not Meant to Protect Pornography." *New York Times,* 7
June 1984, sec. A, 30.

Clifford, Frank. "Council Rejects Anti-Pornography Law." *Los
    Angeles Times,* 22 June 1985, sec. 2, 1, 3.

Report on the Los Angeles City Council rejection of the
antipornography ordinance by an eight-to-four vote. ". . . opponents
argued that the law would lead to censorship and harassment but
offer few benefits not provided by existing laws." The proposal "lost
the support of women's groups which had been among the catalysts
for the measure and which argued that women are victimized by
pornography" when the ordinance was broadened to allow anyone
to sue "providing they were coerced or harmed."

Clifford, Frank. "Disputed Anti-Porn Measure Faces Council Test."
    Los Angeles Times, 21 June 1985, sec. 1, 6.

A report on the antipornography law before the Los Angeles
City Council. Originally patterned after the Indianapolis ordinance,

it was rewritten after a federal judge ruled against it. The current proposal "would allow anyone, under certain conditions, to sue manufacturers, distributors and exhibitors of films or pictures of sexual abuse and debasement of human beings which encourage, incite or instruct in acts of sexual violence or debasement. . . ." Critics of the proposal say the language is too vague.

Clines, Francis S. "A Tale of Two Views on Erotica." *New York Times,* 15 September 1985, sec. A, part 2, 62.
    Clines contrasts the views on pornography of Henry E. Hudson, chairman of the Meese Commission on Pornography, and Dennis Sobin, trade representative of the X–rated entertainment industry in Washington, D.C. Mr. Hudson says the Commission is finding "considerable new information on the commerce and social effects of pornography, ranging from women's concerns to technological changes." Mr. Sobin agrees there have been revolutionary changes in the pornography business, specifically "the soaring use of sexually explicit tape on home video recorders." Questioned whether pornographic material affects human behavior, Mr. Sobin agrees that it does: "People tend to engage in sex because of it."

Cohen, Richard. "Issues Often Viewed Through Special Lens." *Washington Post,* 16 August 1977, sec. C, 1.
    Cohen is critical of the women's movement for defining pornography as a women's issue only. "The thing that bothers me is that all this is coming from people who should be more zealous in protecting everyone's First Amendment rights—including the right of all printed material to find a market. There is more here at stake than simply the women's movement."

Cohen, Richard. "Star of 'Deep Throat' Reveals a Lot About Porn." *Washington Post,* 18 May 1980, sec. C, 1.
    Linda Lovelace's book, *Ordeal* (New York: Berkeley, 1980), prompts Cohen to rethink his attitudes towards pornography. Even though he is a strong supporter of the First Amendment, the book makes him realize that pornography reinforces bigoted stereotypes. "It [pornography] may, in fact, be linked to violence directed at women because all stereotypes tend to dehumanize, making objects out of people—hate objects or sex objects."

Connell, Rich. "County to Explore Adoption of Tough
   Pornography Law." *Los Angeles Times*, 27 February 1985,
   sec. 2, 1, 3.
   News report on the antipornography ordinance, similar to the
Indianapolis ordinance, proposed to the Los Angeles Board of
Supervisors by the County Commission for Women. Two supervisors "argued for immediate approval of the ordinance, but could not
muster a needed third vote." Speaking in support of the ordinance
were feminist attorney, Gloria Allred, and movie director, Peter
Bogdanovich. Allred said, "Allowing the constant glorification of the
subordination of women through pornography to continue is fundamentally inconsistent with our national commitment to equality."
Another speaker was Libertarian Party activist, Wendy McElroy. She
said the ordinance "suggests that 'women need to be protected from
the consequences of their own actions. . . . this is not a step forward
for women.' "

Connell, Rich. "Showdown on County Anti-Smut Law Put Off."
   Los Angeles Times, 27 March 1985, sec. 2, 3.
   News report on the postponement of the vote on the antipornography ordinance by the Los Angeles County Board of Supervisors. The delay was requested by the County Commission for
Women, who recommended the ordinance to the board. The commission asked for time to respond to the board attorney's opinion
"that the measure would be an unconstitutional impairment of free
speech." A leader of a coalition of feminists against the ordinance
said after the vote to postpone the issue, "We don't want it rewritten.
We want it stopped."

"Council Panel Studies Tough Anti-Porn Law." *Los Angeles Times*,
   16 August 1984, sec. 1, 21.
   Brief report on the hearings being held by the Los Angeles City
Council Public Health, Human Resources, and Senior Citizens
Committee on antipornography legislation similar to that passed in
Indianapolis. Councilman Ernani Bernardi said: "We're talking
about certain types of pornography that depicts [*sic*] violence,
depicts [*sic*] that women are inferior to men, and may be violating
the civil rights of women and all people."

"Debate Persists on Rights and Smut." *New York Times*, 21
    November 1984, sec. A, 17.
    News article on the antipornography measures passed in Indi-
anapolis and Minneapolis and being considered in Suffolk County,
New York; Los Angeles; Madison, Wisconsin; and Des Moines,
Iowa. Supporters of the law are undaunted by Judge Sarah Barker's
ruling in federal district court on the Indianapolis ordinance. Finding the law to be an impermissible encroachment on the First
Amendment, the judge said, "Free speech, rather than being the
enemy, is a long-tested and worthy ally."

Decker, Cathleen. "Feminists Resist Pornography Law." *Los Angeles
    Times*, 16 March 1985, sec. 2, 1.
    Report on a news conference held by a coalition of feminists
opposed to the antipornography ordinance before the Los Angeles
County Board of Supervisors. They requested that the ordinance "be
scrapped because it violates the right of free speech and could be
twisted into banning feminist and sex education books." Defenders
of the ordinance countered that, "Feminists need to care about
equality as much as they care about free speech."

"Defeated by Pornography." *New York Times*, 2 June 1986,
    sec. A, 16.
    Editorial criticizing the Meese Commission report for "relying
on questionable evidence and recklessly encouraging censorship."
The writer goes on to report that Dr. Edward Donnerstein has
termed "bizarre" the commission's use of his research. While ac-
knowledging there is a pornography problem in this country, the
editorial concludes the commission's "cure of censorship is worse
than the disease."
    A response from Rev. Bruce Ritter, a member of the commis-
sion, is in the *Times*, 14 June 1986, 26.

"Demonstration Hits Decision on Obscenity Law." *Washington
    Post*, 14 July 1984, sec. A, 6.
    A short news report on the Minneapolis City Council vote to
delay an ordinance defining pornography as a violation of women's
civil rights which led to a demonstration and twenty-five arrests. The
mayor later vetoed the ordinance citing the needlessness of a costly
legal battle while the Indianapolis ordinance is still pending.

"Council action came three days after a young woman set herself afire in a downtown bookstore to protest pornography. Ruth Christensen was hospitalized in critical condition."

A similar Associated Press report is in the *Los Angeles Times,* 14 July 1984, sec. 1, 11.

Dershowitz, Alan M. "Free-Free-Speech." *New York Times,*
    9 February 1979, sec. A, 31.

Dershowitz, a Harvard law professor, laments the changing climate that now has "our old and dear friends: activists in the women's movement, the civil rights movement and the radical left" opposing the civil libertarians. He is highly critical of the attempt by such groups to ban expressions that are offensive to them. "Indeed, one of the great virtues of the First Amendment is that it does not permit the government to pick and choose among offensive expressions, for if it were to ban expressions that offend one group, then it could not justify refusing to ban expressions offensive to other groups."

"Detailed Descriptions in Pornography Report." *New York Times,*
    27 May 1986, sec. A, 17.

United Press International story on the sexually explicit nature of one section of the U.S. Attorney General's Commission on Pornography final report. The ACLU said "the report will include hundreds of pages of titles and descriptions, including detailed and graphic plot summaries, of books, magazines and videotapes it considers pornographic. There are reportedly no illustrations, however."

Donnerstein, Edward, and Daniel Linz. "Dear Editor." *Village
    Voice,* 6 November 1984, 5.

Donnerstein and Linz write to "correct what we believe to be a false impression" of MacKinnon's and Dworkin's use of their research found in Lisa Duggan's article (see below), "Forbidden Fantasies: Censorship in the Name of Feminism" in the 16 October issue. They believe MacKinnon and Dworkin "have consistently used social psychological research cautiously" and that "they have rightly placed the research in its proper perspective."

Duggan replies that at the Indianapolis ordinance hearings MacKinnon and Donnerstein gave conflicting testimony on this research. "These differences in interpretation are crucial when public policy is being based on them."

"Dorchen Leidholdt vs. Civil Liberties Union." *Gay Community News*, 25 May 1985.

Leidholdt, a founder of Women Against Pornography, debated Natasha Lisman of the Massachusetts Civil Liberties Union at an event sponsored by the Women's National Book Association. "The most striking feature of the debate was what was not discussed. Both speakers disliked pornography; their disagreement was on whether the damage attributed to it is worse than that which results from censorship."

Duggan, Lisa. "The Dubious Porn War Alliance." *Washington Post*, 1 September 1985, sec. C, 1, 4.

Duggan compares and contrasts the feminist and conservative groups fighting pornography. She finds their rhetoric to be the same but their goals to be different. "Conservatives fear pornography undermines the traditional family; anti-porn feminists believe it maintains male domination." She surveys the various solutions to the problem of pornography: zoning laws, stricter obscenity laws, the MacKinnon-Dworkin ordinance, and the formation of the Meese Commission on Pornography. In reviewing the hearings of the commission she believes their recommendation may well be for repressive measures. The danger of this is that "we will lose access to explicit sexual expression, which is a part of human life," and more importantly, "the suppression of pornography could be substituted for demands for more meaningful social change."

Duggan, Lisa. "Forbidden Fantasies: Censorship in the Name of Feminism." *Village Voice*, 16 October 1984, 11–12, 16–17, 42.

A very detailed report on the antipornography legislation in Indianapolis: the background of its development, the unlikely coalitions that garnered support for it, and the "collection of publishers, booksellers, broadcasters, and librarians joined by the ACLU" to stop it. There are details on Indianapolis as a community and how the ordinance evolved from the work of MacKinnon and Dworkin. Criticism by local feminists is described. Duggan concludes: "*No* effort was made to distinguish clearly the feminist from the conservative position. As a result the visibility of reactionary, antifeminist forces was enhanced—exactly the opposite of what MacKinnon intended." See letters in response to this article in the 6 November 1984 *Village Voice*.

Duggan, Lisa, and Ann Snitow. "Porn Law Is About Images, Not Power." ("Viewpoint" column) *Newsday* (New York), 26 September 1984, 65.

Negative view of proposed antipornography legislation in Suffolk County, New York. The writers state that women need the power to run their own lives, not more protective legislation. Duggan and Snitow don't believe that images of violence necessarily lead to actual violence in practice. "A picture of a rape is not a rape." They also say that some sexually explicit material has as much to contribute to women's sexual pleasure as to men's and that laws meant to protect women might in fact harm them.

Dullea, Georgia. "In Feminists' Antipornography Drive, 42nd Street is the Target." *New York Times*, 6 July 1979, sec. A, 12.

A report on the Times Square tours led by Women Against Pornography, which are "a small fund-raiser and a big consciousness-raiser." The tour begins with a slide show at the WAP office, which features how women are pornographically depicted in books, magazines, album covers, posters, and advertising. Two sex "supermarkets," bookstores, and a topless bar are visited on the tour. The tour described by Dullea was led by Susan Brownmiller. On Forty-second Street, Brownmiller commented "on the prurient points of interest, the history of the buildings, the underworld figures who owned them, the wages and working conditions of the women employed there and other facts." On the conflict over First Amendment rights versus suppressing pornography Brownmiller said, "Nowhere is it written that you can exploit a woman's body because of the First Amendment."

Dworkin, Andrea. "Dear Editor." *Village Voice*, 6 November 1984, 5.

Dworkin writes in response to the "Forbidden Fantasy" articles that appeared in the 16 October *Village Voice* (see above). She finds their reporting to contain "mistakes of fact and meaning." She specifically objects to a quote attributed to her in Lisa Duggan's article "Forbidden Fantasies: Censorship in the Name of Feminism." Dworkin concludes: "Your record in reporting the radical feminist critique of pornography is a disgrace. So is the way you deal with me and my work."

Duggan responds that she took the quotation in question from *Off Our Backs*, "a publication which cannot be accused of hostility to radical feminism."

Dworkin, Andrea. "Pornography's Part in Sexual Violence." *Los Angeles Times*, 26 May 1981, sec. 2, 5.

Dworkin writes about the case of three Hartford, Connecticut women who were arrested for pouring blood on pornographic materials at a local store. At their trial, at which Dworkin testified, in their defense, "They claimed that they had acted to prevent a greater crime—the sexual abuse of women and children; that the materials in question contributed materially to sexual violence against women and children; that society had a greater obligation to protect women's lives than dildos." The women were acquitted. She goes on to discuss the growing awareness among women of the role of pornography in sexual abuse and "the refusal, especially among liberals, to believe that pornography has any real relationship to sexual violence."

Letters, most disagreeing with this article, are printed in the *Los Angeles Times*, 6 June 1981, sec. 2, 2.

Ehrenreich, Barbara. "Pornography as Paradox." *New York Times Book Review*, 29 September 1985, 50.

A review of Varda Burstyn's *Women Against Censorship* (Vancouver, B.C.: Douglas and McIntyre, 1985) and *Magic Mommas, Trembling Sisters, Puritans and Perverts*, (Trumansburg, N.Y.: Crossing Press, 1985) by Joanna Russ. Ehrenreich comments on the intrafeminist fights over the antipornography movement, the "unseemly" alliance of feminists and the radical right, and the dangers of censorship. She believes this alliance may have been the motivation for the authors of these two books. She summarizes the arguments of Russ and Burstyn by saying no one can agree on what pornography is, what good it would do to get rid of it, and that, in fact, it might be dangerous to do so. These two books referred to are included in the "Books" section.

In the *New York Times Book Review* of 10 November 1985 (page 53) Catharine MacKinnon and Andrea Dworkin criticize this review.

Ennis, Kathleen. "Feminists Take Protest to 14th Street."
Washington Post, 3 August 1980, sec. B, 7.
News report on a demonstration sponsored by D.C. Feminists Against Pornography. The group of about seventy people picketed adult book stores and movie houses. The president of the group said, "Pornography is a message of domination of women by men." The demonstration attracted jeers and supporters of pornography. "Dressed as a prostitute, an owner of an adult novelty shop handed out a flyer called 'Erotic Consumers Rights.' "

"Excerpts From Final Report of Attorney General's Panel on
Pornography." *New York Times,* 10 July 1986, sec. B, 7.
Two sections from the final report of Meese Commission on Pornography are excerpted: the section "The Question of Harm" on the topics of sexually violent material, nonviolent material, and nondegrading materials, and the section covering recommendations for changes in federal laws.

"FBI Director Is Content With Antismut Arsenal." *Washington Post,*
21 June 1985, sec. A, 16.
A news story on the testimony of FBI Director William H. Webster before the Attorney General's Commission on Pornography. Webster testified he sees "no need for new weapons against smut." He is satisfied with "measures enacted last year involving organized crime and wire-taps." Surgeon General C. Everett Koop "offered his agency's aid in determining whether there is a direct link between pornography and antisocial behavior." A spokesman for the ACLU "voiced hope that the commission will ignore 'moral mob rule' in deciding its recommendations."

"Feminists vs. Pornography." *Christian Science Monitor,* 21 July
1977, 28.
An editorial commending feminists for "adding a welcome thrust to the antipornography fight apparently growing in all walks

of life." Suggests an antipornography drive should be on the agenda of the national women's conference to be held in November. Goes on to caution that the fight should not only be against hard-core pornography, but also the "lesser but increasing doses" found on television. "The feminists now in the fray should have the support of all those who realize that the degradation of one sex degrades the other, too."

A reader comments in the 16 August 1977, issue of the *Monitor* that the "women's libbers" are trying to steal the thunder of Phyllis Schlafly's Eagle Forum "by pretending to oppose pornography."

Feshbach, Seymour. "Mixing Sex With Violence—A Dangerous
    Alchemy." *New York Times,* 3 August 1980, sec. D, 29.
    A brief synopsis by Feshbach on the research he has conducted with Neil Malamuth on the depiction of violence in pornography. He does not propose censorship, but a "greater consciousness of the possibility that when violence is fused with sex, we have a potentially dangerous form of alchemy."

"Final Report on Pornography Prompts Debate." *New York Times,*
    13 July 1986, sec. E, 4.
    Brief summary of the recommendations in the final report of the U.S. Attorney General's Commission on Pornography, along with the reactions of Barry Lynn of the ACLU and Bruce Hallman of Christian Voice.

Friedan, Betty. "How to Get the Women's Movement Moving
    Again." *New York Times Magazine,* 3 November 1985, 26–28,
    66–67, 84–85, 89, 98, 106–108.
    A personal observation on the past accomplishments of the women's movement. She says there is more to be done but the movement is in trouble and needs to get back on course. She makes frequent reference to and deplores "the preoccupation with pornography and other sexual diversions that do not affect most women's lives."

Gamarekian, Barbara. "Report Draws Strong Praise and Criticism."
    New York Times, 10 July 1986, sec. B, 7.
    Gamarekian reports on the reactions of various organizations and individuals to the U.S. Attorney General's Commission on

Pornography's final report. Bruce Hallman of Christian Voice, John Harrington of Americans for Constitutional Freedom, Christie Hefner of Playboy Enterprises, and a statement from the National Organization of Women are among those quoted. Linda Marciano said "she was 'proud to see my government pick up the ball.'"

Gardner, Sandra. "New Jerseyans." *New York Times,* 8 September 1985, sec. 11NJ, 6.
Brief story on Professor Katherine Ellis of Rutgers University and founder of the Feminist Anti-Censorship Taskforce. "People who support the proposed antipornography legislation certainly feel that we're not feminists, not sympathetic to women's suffering. They think we're getting into bed with the pornographers." She thinks "they're getting into bed with the conservatives."

Goldstein, Al. "Cable TV's Shame: 'Gore-nography.'" *New York Times,* 3 July 1984, sec. A, 15.
An essay criticizing cable television stations for showing horror movies such as *Prom Night, Psycho II,* and *Cujo* on the eight o'clock movie when children could be watching. Goldstein believes "horror films are far more damaging representations of the female role in society than are porn films."

Goldstein, Richard. "Pornography and Its Discontents." *Village Voice,* 16 October 1984, 19–22, 44.
Goldstein discusses several pornographic films and the fantasies they reflect. "Even if pornography were banned as a clear and present danger, we would still be left with the content of our fantasies, and our fantasies would still be laced with those images of 'submission and display' by which anti-porn activists define pornography." He then describes a film that centers entirely on violence to women. He concludes, "Pornography is misogynist because the culture is misogynist, not the other way around." Although he can understand the rage such films can cause women, he writes: "Trying to destroy dangerous art is like shooting at a rainbow; you can never hit the source. No sooner do you succeed at banning one offensive work than others, more covert, arise."
See letters in response to this article in the *Village Voice,* 6 November 1984.

Goleman, Daniel. "Researchers Dispute Pornography Report On
    Its Use of Data." *New York Times,* 17 May 1986, sec. A, 1, 35.
    A draft of the Meese Commission report drew expressions of
shock from some of the social scientists it cites for stating there is a
causal relationship between pornography and sexual violence.
Edward Donnerstein said, " 'These conclusions seem bizarre to me.' "
The commission executive director said "the panel did not rely only
on the research of social scientists, but, instead, sought a wide range
of testimony from law-enforcement officers, members of the clergy
and others." Commission member Dr. Judith Becker also disagrees
with this conclusion. "She said she would write a dissenting opinion."
    Letters in response to this article are in the *New York Times,*
7 June 1986, 26.

Goodman, Ellen. "Pornography Is Harmful, But. . . ." *Washington
    Post,* 14 January 1984, sec. A, 21.
    Goodman briefly reviews the research of Donnerstein and the
Minneapolis antipornography ordinance vetoed by the mayor last
week. "In many ways, the Minneapolis ordinance is an appealing
attack on an appalling problem." Yet, she feels such legislation could
easily "strangle free expression." "In its present form, this is still a
shaky piece of law."
    This article was reprinted in the *Los Angeles Times,* 17 January
1984, sec. 2, 5.

Goodman, Ellen. "Protecting Free Speech And Our Children."
    Washington Post, 19 May 1981, sec. A, 13.
    Goodman first considers a New York Court of Appeals ruling
reversing the conviction of a Times Square bookstore owner for
selling child pornography. "This decision is likely to become an
emotional flash point in the heated, lengthy debate between the
value of the First Amendment and the evil of pornography. . . ." She
then goes on to report just such a debate that took place between
Andrea Dworkin and Harvard Law School Professor, Alan Dershowitz. "Dworkin condemned the anti-female politics of pornography
and its deliberate systematic violence against women and children.
Dershowitz condemned the dangers of banning: who is to do the
banning?" Goodman sees the merit of both arguments as the title of
this essay indicates.

Goodman, Walter. "Battle on Pornography Spurred by New
 Tactics." *New York Times*, 3 July 1984, sec. A, 8.
Review of the efforts to ban pornography that have brought
feminists and conservatives together. Includes the research results of
Dr. Diana E. H. Russell of Mills College, that "a large percentage of
the male population has a propensity to rape." Also quotes Professor
Edward Donnerstein that his research has "been 'misused' by opponents of pornography. If you take the violent content out of
pornographic films and leave only the explicit sex, there is no effect
[on behavior]."

Goodman, Walter. "Pornography: Esthetics to Censorship
 Debated." *New York Times*, 13 August 1984, sec. C, 21.
A news report of a panel discussion on "What is pornography"
sponsored by *Harper's* magazine. The panelists were Al Goldstein,
publisher of *Screw* magazine; Susan Brownmiller; Erica Jong; Midge
Decter; Jean Elshtain, who teaches political science at the University
of Massachusetts; and Aryeh Neier, former executive director of the
American Civil Liberties Union. The "two-hour discussion covered
everything from esthetics to censorship, from the causes of violence
against women and the meaning of sexual liberation to the shortcomings of uptight intellectuals." Miss Brownmiller was without
supporters on the panel when she argued that pornography was
humiliating to women and led to violence against women and when
she sought to restrict access to pornography. To her complaint that
pornography was antifemale propaganda Mr. Goldstein replied,
"Tough!" "Such propaganda," he said, "had the same right to exist as
any other kind of propaganda—That's democracy." He offered Miss
Brownmiller a "one-way plane ticket to Cuba."

Gould, Lois. "Pornography for Women." *The New York Times
 Magazine*, 2 March 1979, 2.
Tells about a porn shop with a "women also welcome" sign
which the author says indicates that the pornography industry is
trying to "go co-ed." Repeats the reasons for pornography's appeal
to men, as explained by some social scientists. Describes pornographic books, films, magazines now meant to appeal to women and
women's apparent lack of sustained interest in them. Cites studies of
male and female sexual thoughts and feelings after viewing pornography.

"A Greater Harm." *Los Angeles Times*, 25 February 1986, sec. 2, 4.
An editorial in support of the U.S. Supreme Court ruling against the Indianapolis antipornography ordinance. "This ordinance was a bad idea from the outset, and it was clear that it would not survive a constitutional challenge." Notes that the Los Angeles County Board of Supervisors shelved a similar proposal. "Instead, the supervisors created a Task Force on Pornography, which is now trying to come up with another plan for limiting the availability of pornographic material. So far it hasn't come up with any."

Gruson, Lindsay. "Pornography Bill is Issue in Suffolk." *New York Times,* 13 November 1984, sec. B, 2.
A news report on the antipornography bill introduced in the Suffolk County, New York legislature by Michael D'Andre. D'Andre, who opposes the equal rights amendment, homosexual rights, and abortion, counters charges of censorship with the statement: "I'm willing to think for the majority. The majority rules." County legislators are under great pressure to vote for the bill, as no one wants to be charged with supporting pornography. All members of the county legislature are up for reelection next year.

Hafhill, Robert. "Speaking Out: On Anti-Porn Efforts and Gay Male Separatism." *Gay Community News,* 26 May 1984, 5.
Hafhill says the antipornography movement separates gays and lesbian feminists because proposed ordinances and other actions are anti-gay. He says the actions of a majority of lesbians in the Minneapolis area have led to the "arrest of nearly 3,500 gays in adult bookstores and elsewhere in the last three-and-a-half years." He cites a variety of meetings and quotations to prove his point that the antipornography movement is anti-gay and that it leads to separation and should lead gay men "to move against the source of the pressure in the feminist, lesbian and neighborhood movements."

Hager, Philip. "Court Voids Law on Pornography." *Los Angeles Times.* 25 February 1985, sec. 1, 10.
Report on the U.S. Supreme Court six-to-three ruling affirming the federal appeals court decision that the Indianapolis antipornography ordinance was a violation of free speech. Hager notes that the Los Angeles County Board of Supervisors and the Los

Angeles City Council had rejected similar proposals. Gives a brief history of the Indianapolis case *Hudnut* v. *American Booksellers,* 85-1090.

Harper, Phillip Brian. "Gay Man and Pornography." *Gay Community News,* 2 October 1982, 8.

This article is a conversation between the author and another *GCN* writer named Metzel. It only briefly deals with the feminist antipornography movement, but is included here because it comes from a different perspective—gay male—than other articles included. There is some commentary on books by Dworkin and Steinem and on Women Against Pornography.

Headden, Susan. "Judge Tosses Out City's Porn Law." *Indianapolis Star,* 24 November 1984, 1.

Story on Judge Sarah Evans Barker's ruling that the Indianapolis antipornography ordinance was in violation of the First Amendment. The ordinance is described and the judge's reasoning is reported in detail.

Hentoff, Nat. "Civil-Rights Censors." *Washington Post,* 14 September 1985, sec. A, 19.

An essay on the legal battles over the Indianapolis ordinance, quoting from the decisions of Federal District Judge Barker and Judge Frank Easterbrook of the Seventh Circuit Court—who both ruled against the ordinance. Hentoff also brings in the *amicus* brief filed by FACT.

Hentoff, Nat. "A Hoosier Madisonian." *Washington Post,* 29 November 1984, sec. A, 27.

An essay on Judge Sarah Evans Barker of the federal district court, and the ruling against the Indianapolis antipornography ordinance. Some people were concerned "that a Reagan appointee to the federal bench was going to make the first constitutional judgment anywhere in the nation on a wholly new approach to banning alleged pornography." On 19 November, in a fifty-eight page decision, Judge Barker "demolished the 'civil rights' approach to suppressing speech designed by . . . Catharine MacKinnon." Hentoff quotes from the decision.

Hentoff, Nat. "Is the First Amendment Dangerous to Women?"
    Village Voice, 16 October 1984, 14; "Censorship Unlimited."
    Village Voice, 23 October 1984, 8; "Equal-Opportunity
    Banning." *Village Voice,* 30 October 1984, 8.

A series of three articles on the MacKinnon-Dworkin antipornography ordinance. Hentoff strongly opposes the ordinance for
vagueness of language and lack of clear guidelines for enforcement.
"The scope of the material, in all forms of expression, that the
MacKinnon-Dworkin guillotine would remove from all eyes is, as
Thomas Emerson puts it, 'breathtaking.' " He sees such legislation as
opening the door for many other groups, such as blacks, Jews,
Asians, and Hispanics, to request the suppression of material on the
same civil rights claim. He also questions the reliance of MacKinnon-Dworkin on the research of Professor Edward Donnerstein.
"He [Donnerstein] does not find a connection between violent
pornography and actual violence against women. And, he adds, no
other researcher has."

See letters in response in the 6 November 1984 issue of the
Village Voice.

Hentoff, Nat. "The Lust to Censor." *Washington Post,* 19 May
    1981, sec. A, 13.

To support the title of this essay, Hentoff cites two recent
examples of censorship. The first was at the Franklin Pierce Law
Center in Concord, New Hampshire, where the students voted to
ban *Playboy, Penthouse,* and *Hustler* from the cooperative bookstore.
". . . as might be expected, this new Yankee legion of decency was
powered by feminists." One of the defenders of the action said it was
not a First Amendment issue. "It was a question of marketing policy
rather than constitutional law."

The second example was at the University of Wisconsin in
Madison. A group of women persuaded the dean of the School of
Education to remove a book of lithographs from an art exhibit. They
"pointed out to him that the lithographs, degrading women as they
did, constituted sexual harassment." Hentoff wonders what this
means for "the future of free expression in the academy under this
innovative standard for policing (but not, of course, censoring)
antisocial materials."

Hentoff, Nat. "War on Pornography: The First Casualty is Free
   Speech." *Washington Post,* 31 August 1984, sec. A, 21.
   Hentoff surveys the appeal of the Indianapolis antipornography
ordinance to other cities. Public officials in Des Moines; Detroit;
Suffolk County, New York; Columbus; Omaha; Cincinnati; St.
Louis; and Madison, Wisconsin are waiting for the court to rule on
the Indianapolis law. The Iowa Civil Liberties Union "predicts the
Des Moines City Council, if given a chance, will unanimously pass a
civil rights anti-pornography bill, and Mayor Peter Crivaro will sign
it." The mayor is quoted as saying, " '. . . we must do what is in the
best interest of the majority.' If James Madison heard that one, he
might well burst into tears."

Herlihy, Sear. "Anti-Censorship Forum." *Gay Community News,* 13
   April 1985, 10.
   The report of a lecture by Lisa Duggan, one of the organizers of
FACT. She says, "It looks like the women's movement is backing off
from supporting anti-pornography legislation." She notes incidents
of cooperation between feminists and the right wing and points out
that the right wing and the feminist opponents of pornography
differ sharply in their world views.

Hill, Morton, S.J. "To Women Degraded by Porn: Ring the Bell."
   Variety, 3 January 1979, 16, 46.
   President of Morality In Media, Inc. comments on the march of
5,000 women in San Francisco through the pornography district
and other strategies used by feminists against pornography (leaflets,
picketing, boycotts) and says they are not enough; laws should be
used instead. He then criticizes those officials he believes should be
using the laws to stop pornography. Hill describes the activities of
his organization, and its participation in the New York University
Law School forum, "Obscenity: Degradation of Women Versus
Right of Free Speech."

Hirshson, Paul. "Antipornography Vote Appears Headed for
   Defeat in Cambridge." *Boston Globe,* 9 November 1985, 23.
   A news report on the Cambridge, Massachusetts, antipornog-
raphy ordinance, modeled after the MacKinnon-Dworkin law, that

was on the ballot in the 5 November election. With half the ballots counted, the referendum was losing by 1,400 votes.

Hirshson, Paul. "Antismut Law Looks Dead in Cambridge." *Boston Globe,* 10 November 1985, 33, 37.

A news report on the Cambridge antipornography ordinance that is losing by a three to two margin, as the votes continue to be counted. Ellen Corey of Women Against Pornography said her group was not conceding defeat. "Our support will grow in time," she said.

A condensed report on the Cambridge election appears in the *Boston Globe* on 11 November 1985, 21.

Hirshon, Paul. "Cambridge Ends Counting; 4 New Officials." *Boston Globe,* 12 November 1985, 45.

Brief news report on the completion of the counting of votes in Cambridge. The antipornography referendum lost by more than 3,600 votes.

Hirshson, Paul. "Council Vote Blocks Ballot Question on Pornography in Cambridge." *Boston Globe,* 11 September 1985, 24.

News report on the Cambridge City Council five-to-four vote to reject putting an antipornography measure on the ballot in November, "despite more than 5,200 signatures on a petition favoring it." Sponsors of the measure, Women's Alliance Against Pornography, said they would await the outcome of a reconsideration vote next week before deciding on further action. The Cambridge Commission on the Status of Women also voted disapproval of the measure.

Hirshson, Paul. "Pornography Fighter Backs Cambridge Plan." *Boston Globe,* 6 October 1985, 42.

A report on Catharine MacKinnon's visit to Harvard Law School to lend her support to the antipornography referendum that will appear on the 5 November city ballot. The issue "has put many in this diverse and university-oriented city into a dilemma." The head of the Civil Liberties Union of Massachusetts said of opposition to the ordinance: " 'It's important for people to see that it's not a pro-pornography position, but an anticensorship issue.' " WAAP, which sponsors the referendum, "has about 20 to 30 people in its core group and about 300 supporters," said the Civil Liberties Union spokesperson.

Holt, Joyce Sunila. "DePalma's Rage to Sow a Porn Plot." *Los Angeles Times,* 4 March 1984, Calendar, 37.

Holt responds to an *Esquire* magazine interview with Brian DePalma, in which he describes his next project as a "hard-core 'pornographic suspense' movie." Holt does not believe DePalma is breaking new ground, as he claims. "Few trends are more obvious than the backlash against feminism that has spawned the violent, misogynist rock videos, and that partly accounts for the brisk sales of pornographic home videocassettes." She envisions the publicity DePalma will receive when the movie comes out. The press will call his "camera tricks 'genius' and women will watch the whole circus in sad silence, hoping against hope that if they don't go see the movie, it won't hurt them."

"How Not to Fight Pornography." *New York Times,* 24 December 1978, sec. D, 10.

An editorial on the New York University conference Obscenity: Degradation of Women Versus Right of Free Speech. Quotes several of the feminist speakers without identifying them, and describes one of them as overwrought. The writers feel a "sounder approach to a nasty business" is that put forth by NOW's president, Eleanor Smeal. She "emphasizes the need for making men as well as women aware of the sadism that is built into much pornography and encouraging them to take 'direct action,' such as boycotts of the worst offenders."

Hunter, Nan D. "Anti-Pornography Measure Could Backfire on Women." *Los Angeles Times,* 21 March 1985, sec. 2, 5.

Hunter believes the antipornography bill before the Los Angeles County Board of Supervisors "represents a dangerous and misguided strategy for the women's movement. . . ." She agrees that women do live with the threat of violence, "but the causes . . . are deep-seated, structural and complex. Whatever role images may play, there is no reason to believe that sexual images are at the core." She sees the "quick-fix appeal" of such ordinances "but their promise to stop men's abuse of women is illusory and dangerous."

Hunter, Nan. "Power and Pornography." *Village Voice,*
    27 November 1984, 51.
    A rebuttal to the column by Janella Miller (see below) in the 6 November issue, Hunter believes Miller is incorrect in her claim "that the ordinance consists of narrow and specific language." She believes the MacKinnon-Dworkin ordinance will give greater power to the judicial system. "It will be judges, not feminists, who decide which images are permitted expression."

"Indiana Porn." *Washington Post,* 12 May 1984, sec. A, 14.
    An editorial labeling "wrongheaded" the antipornography ordinance passed by the Indianapolis City Council and signed by Mayor William Hudnut. They believe it allows "exactly the kind of censorship the Constitution prohibits. . . . Feminist groups concerned about the impact of this material should keep up the effort to instruct the public on the harm it inflicts on those exploited and to bring economic pressure to bear on those who profit in the $7 billion-a-year industry."

"Indianapolis Approves Antipornography Law." *New York Times,*
    24 April 1984, sec. A, 17.
    An Associated Press news story on the passage of the antipornography ordinance by the Indianapolis City-County Council. The vote was twenty-four to five.

Irvine, Janice. "Pornography—What's Best for Women." *Gay
    Community News,* 3 August 1985, 8.
    A report on the *amicus* brief submitted by FACT in April to the Seventh Circuit Court of Appeals in Indiana where the MacKinnon-Dworkin ordinance is under review. "The FACT brief centers around two major arguments: First Amendment rights and equal protection principles." It contends the language of the ordinance is so vague it could lead to suppression of any sexually explicit images. In its equal protection arguments, FACT finds the ordinance to be sexist. " 'In treating women as a special class, it repeats the errors of earlier protectionist legislation which gave women no significant benefits and denied their equality.'"

Irvine, Janice, and Sue Hyde. "Carole Vance: Porn, Politics, and
Pleasure." *Gay Community News,* 23 February 1985, 8–10.

An interview with Carole Vance who served as the academic
coordinator of the Scholar and the Feminist IX conference at
Barnard. The interviewers state that it is clear that Vance's commitment "to broadening the dialogue about sex rang through the
discussion as a continuous refrain." Vance says she believes the
antiporn people are devoting all their effort to getting rid of images
instead of "elaborating on what we know and are interested in—
what we find pleasurable." In addition to describing her role in the
Scholar and Feminist IX conference Towards a Politics of Sexuality,
held at Barnard College in New York City in 1982, Vance discusses
her fight against the antipornography legislation in Suffolk County.
A founder of FACT, she describes the right-wing efforts in Suffolk
County, New York, which provided an impetus for the formation of
this group.

Irwin, Victoria. "A Conflict of Images; Fashion Magazines: What
Do They Say About Women?" *Christian Science Monitor,*
6 October1981, 18, midwestern edition.

A discussion of the double message coming from fashion
magazines. On the one hand there are more articles about independent women, and at the same time "a second image of woman as a
sexual object and seductress," presented by some of the fashion
advertising, photos, and editorial copy. Examples of this dichotomy
are given from *Vogue, Harper's Bazaar,* and *Mademoiselle.*

"Is New Action Needed on Pornography?" *New York Times,*
23 June 1985, sec. D, 24.

Excerpts from an interview with Henry E. Hudson, chairman
of the U.S. Attorney General's Commission on Pornography. Questioned about the makeup of the commission Hudson responded: "I
think it is a very well-balanced commission. We have behavioral
scientists, people in law enforcement, people who are associated with
the women's side of the issues, physicians and psychologists." The
interviewer pointed out that critics note there is only one representative of the media and three members with a background in law
enforcement on the panel. Asked if there should have been a better
balance, Hudson said, "No."

Jackman, Frank. "Justices XXX Out a Sex Law." *Daily News* (New
York), 25 February 1986, 7.

A law that would have defined pornography as sex discrimination and made porn producers, distributors and exhibitors subject to
civil lawsuits was ruled unconstitutional on 24 February by the U.S.
Supreme Court. The justices delivered their decision without opinion, upholding lower court rulings that said the Indianapolis statute
interfered with free speech. This news article reports the chronology
in court of the Indianapolis ordinance and some of the background
of its supporters.

Jacoby, Susan. "Hers." *New York Times,* 26 January 1978, sec. C, 2.

Jacoby, who calls herself a "First Amendment junkie," discusses
the feminist arguments for controls on pornography. She believes
censorship of pornography cannot be conducted on any more
rational basis than other types of censorship. "They [feminists] want
to use the power of the state to accomplish what they have been
unable to achieve in the marketplace of ideas for ages."

Japenga, Ann. "Sex-Violence Research: He Takes a Feminist
Approach." *Los Angeles Times,* 6 January 1984, sec. 5, 1, 14.

Japenga reports on the research of Neil Malamuth on the
relationship of violent pornography and violence to women. He
found "certain types of violent porn do encourage attitudes of
violence against women." In England and New Zealand his research
has been used to justify censorship of part of films. " 'In some ways it
[the censorship] was gratifying.' Malamuth said, 'but the whole issue
of censorship raises questions for me.' " His current research is "to
see whether a propensity to rape also manifests itself in day-to-day
behavior such as dating and conversational patterns." Malamuth
hopes his work will "help reduce the incidence of sexual assault."

Kain, Kate, et al. "A Feminist Report From the Front Lines of the
War on Pornography." *San Francisco Bay Guardian,* 23
November 1978, 5.

Report on the "Feminist Perspectives in Pornography" conference held in San Francisco, 17–19 November 1978. The 350
participants began "with the basic assumption that all pornography
is harmful and degrading to women and children, and should be

eliminated." Includes brief reports on some of the workshops, such as "Children and Pornography," "Disability and Pornography," and "Feminist Perspectives: Pornography and the First Amendment." Also includes a description of San Francisco's Women Against Violence in Pornography and Media–sponsored Take Back the Night march on 18 November in which 5,000 people participated.

Karkabi, Barbara. "Seminar Addresses Pornography." *Houston Chronicle,* 25 March 1985, sec. 5, 2.
    Report of a conference, sponsored by the Houston Area Women's Center, called "Pornography and Violence Against Women: A Feminist Perspective." Speakers included Robin Morgan, lawyers Marian Rosen and Nikki Van Hightower, and Edward Donnerstein, whose area of research includes pornography and media effects on behavior and attitudes.

Kendrick, Walter. "Prudes and Prejudice: The Meese Commission's Dirty Mind." *Village Voice Literary Supplement,* September 1986, 10–12.
    Kendrick's essay is a joint book review of Susanne Kappeler's *The Pornography of Representation* (Minneapolis: University of Minnesota Press, 1986), Philip Nobile and Eric Nadler's *United States of America vs. Sex* (New York: Minotaur Press, 1986), Barry Lynn's *Polluting the Censorship Debate* (Washington, D.C.: American Civil Liberties Union, 1986) and U.S. Attorney General's Commission on Pornography *Final Report,* (Washington, D.C.: Department of Justice, 1986).
    He characterizes Lynn's book as "the ACLU's 188-page rebuttal (and thorough demolition) of the commission's methodology and findings." Nobile and Nadler, editors at *Forum,* record the operation of the commission hearings. "The result is an efficiently written, often very funny volume that makes a nice companion piece to *Polluting*." Kendrick's harshest criticism is for the commission's report. He supplies a brief history of antismut crusaders beginning with Lord Chief Justice Sir Alexander Cockburn and Anthony Comstock. He finds the commission's report not a very great departure from these earlier opinions. "It's ironic (and terribly sad) that the label 'feminism' is being attached to the same old lust for power. Instead of undertaking the strenuous, time-consuming task

of reforming social attitudes, Dworkin and company prefer the shortcut of tyranny. The deplorable thing is that too many suffering women see the promise of freedom—in what would amount to just an exchange of masters." Kendrick finds Susanne Kappeler's book to be "an intermittently incisive study that collapses, finally under the weight of its own bloated rhetoric."

Klemesrud, Judy. "Bill on Pornography Opposed." *New York Times,* 14 June 1985, sec. A, 18.

Report on Women Against Pornography's opposition to New York Assembly Bill 3883, the "brown-wrapper bill," which would force sellers of pornographic magazines to wrap up their covers or sell them from under the counter. Dorchin Leidholdt, founder of Women Against Pornography, said of the bill, "Our organization opposes this bill because, in spite of the good intentions behind its drafting and passage, it utterly fails to address and provide a remedy for the harm of pornography." The bill was passed by the New York Legislature. Governor Mario Cuomo had not yet received it.

Letters in response to this article, both critical of the position of Women Against Pornography, appeared in the 1 July 1985, sec. A, 14, and 11 July 1985, sec. A, 22 issues of the *New York Times.* They were written by New York Assemblyman, Daniel L. Feldman, and *Penthouse* Chairman, Robert Guccione, respectively.

Klemesrud, Judy. "Joining Hands in the Fight Against Pornography." *New York Times,* 26 August 1985, sec. B, 7.

Asked about the criticism she has received for forming alliances with conservative groups to fight pornography, Andrea Dworkin responded: " 'I think its been terrifically distorted. There hasn't been any institutional support from the right wing, no money, no political support and no intervention in litigation.' " She is critical of " 'organized feminism' for not taking a stronger stand against pornography." The article also includes the views of John Stottenberg who works with Dworkin on the antipornography movement, and their participation in an antipornography march in New Orleans.

Klemesrud, Judy. "Lolita Syndrome Is Denounced." *New York Times,* 3 March 1981, sec. B, 14.

Report of a news conference sponsored by Women Against Pornogrpahy to announce their intention to picket the Broadway production of *Lolita*. They object to the eroticized images of little girls in the play, as well as in advertising and movies. Said one participant: " 'The play trivializes, and thus legitimizes, the exploitation of children and violence against women at a time when conscious men and women are uniting to expose these evils.' "

Klemesrud, Judy. "Women, Pornography, Free Speech: A Fierce Debate at N.Y.U." *New York Times*, 4 December 1978, sec. D, 10.

A report on the colloquium on "Obscenity: Degradation of Women Versus Right of Free Speech" held at New York University School of Law, 2 December 1978. The purpose of the meeting, as planners explained, was "to study the question of how to mitigate the adverse effects of pornography on society without offending the First Amendment." Speakers such as Andrea Dworkin, Susan Brownmiller, and Herald Price Fahringer, general counsel for the First Amendment Lawyers' Association, are quoted.

Kristof, Nicholas D. "X-Rated Industry In a Slump." *New York Times*, 5 October 1986, sec. 3, 1, 6.

A report on the decline of profits in the pornography industry. Several factors for this decline are discussed, including "an unlikely alliance of conservatives and feminists [which] has persuaded many retailers to stop carrying adult magazines and videos." An unknown factor for the industry is the growing number of women who rent X–rated videos. "A recent survey of 500 retailers found that women rented 32 percent of all X–rated videos, while men rented 37 percent; heterosexual couples rented the balance."

Kurtz, Howard. "New War on Pornography. Librarians Argue With Preachers Over City Law." *Washington Post*, 29 July 1984, sec. A, 4.

A description of the "battle over the nation's first ordinance that defines pornography as a violation of women's civil rights" in Indianapolis. Views of the mayor of Indianapolis are reported as are the views of those who fear the implications of this legislation for all published materials. The hearings are described in detail as are some of the participants. The suit was filed by plaintiffs ranging from the American Booksellers Association to the local Video Shack against the MacKinnon-Dworkin ordinance passed by the Indianapolis City

Council in May. Sheila Suess Kennedy, counsel for the plaintiffs, said
" 'I don't like it when people try to ban books in the name of
feminism. I consider myself a feminist, and to use feminism to justify
an outrageous attack on freedom of thought and expression really
makes me angry.' " Indianapolis Mayor William H. Hudnut III
believes the law can succeed in halting the spread of pornographic
materials. "However, even the law's supporters can't agree on how
far it extends."

Kurtz, Howard. "Pornography Panel's Objectivity Disputed:
    Critics Call Meese Commission Overzealous." *Washington Post*,
    15 October 1985, sec. A, 4.
    A report on the hearings and composition of the U.S. Attorney
General's Commission on Pornography. At each hearing, victims of
sexual abuse relate their stories. "Many experts on both sides of the
question say such anecdotal tales of woe prove nothing about the
effect of sexually explicit material." Commission member Judith
Becker says of such testimony, "As a scientist, it's been very difficult
for me to see a very clear cause-and-effect relationship" with pornography. Edward Donnerstein believes it is impossible to prove a link
between pornography and sexual crimes. "The evidence just isn't
that clear cut."
    The article also details criticism of the composition of the
commission; it is "heavily weighted toward law enforcement," and of
its chairman, Henry E. Hudson. Says Burton Joseph, counsel to
Playboy Enterprises, "I don't think Chairman Hudson was chosen
because he had an open mind toward the value of sexually explicit
materials."

Lederer, Laura J. "Pornography Is a Social Carcinogen." *Los Angeles
    Times*, 9 October 1985, sec. 2, 5.
    Lederer believes a direct link between pornography and sexual
crimes may never be scientifically proven. She goes on to describe
two research projects that take a different approach to the subject.
Dr. Ann Burgess is studying convicted sex criminals for what they
have in common. "When asked to rank their sexual interests, pornography ranked highest (87 percent). . . ." Judith Reisman of
American University is doing an analysis of the content of *Playboy*,
Penthouse, and *Hustler* in an effort to know exactly what "kind of

'education' our boys and men are getting." Lederer feels "Men who care about our society (and many who read soft-core pornography pride themselves on their politics and their concern for the health of our society) should consider giving up pornography—much the way one might give up heavy drinking at 'happy hour' to prevent car accidents. . . ."

Lederer, Laura. "Pornography: Think About It." *San Francisco Chronicle,* 14 July 1985, "This World" section, 20.
   Lederer reports that researchers at American University are cataloging activities involving children, crime, and violence in three of the largest pornography magazines—*Playboy, Penthouse,* and *Hustler.* The "so-called soft core pornography magazines are read widely—200 million copies annually, not counting the way they are passed from hand to hand." "For years," says Lederer, "law enforcement officials have been reporting that they find sexually explicit materials, including soft core pornography, at the scene of large numbers of severely violent crime." Lederer says, "The question is not 'Does pornography cause sexual violence?' For, as long as we frame our discussion in terms of cause and effect, we are participating in a 'scientific' game that has no real end." Lederer says that men who care about social issues should consider giving up pornography. "Social change comes because individuals choose to make the world a better place to live."

Levine, Judith. "Perils of Desire." *Voice Literary Supplement.* 12 March 1985, 1, 12–15.
   This is a lengthy review of Carole S. Vance's *Pleasure and Danger* (Boston: Routledge & Kegan Paul, 1984), which records the Barnard Scholar and the Feminist IX conference. Levine finds the book to be "well written and well edited, catholic in substance and style, often ground-breaking, and at times visionary." The problem she has with the contributors to this book, and others in what she labels the "prosex" camp in the debate on feminist sexuality, is the reluctance to actually deal with the issues of danger and violence. "But I am concerned that a fear of treading on these murky issues of violence has created a disturbing ridigity and unresponsiveness within prosex." She believes the antipornography movement has gathered supporters because it is actively doing something.

"Carrying the banner of sexual pleasure, prosex must show itself to be serious about sexual danger, too. I want a democracy of sexual practice—but I also long to take back the slogan, 'Take Back the Night.' "

Lewis, Stephen. "Long Island Opinion: Pornography and the Issues Facing Suffolk." *New York Times*, 13 January 1985, sec. 11LI, 18.

An essay discussing the current antipornography efforts in Suffolk County, Long Island and Indianapolis. Lewis opposes these efforts to regulate such a subjective issue. "We may wish that all abhorrent actions disappear, along with their corollary images, but to translate that wish into legislation that aims only at the images, and not the substance, is a dangerous distortion." He also points out the lack of clear evidence linking pornography and violent crimes against women, and the fact that pornography is not the only available material offensive to women or other groups.

Lindsay, Leon. "Proposed Law Would Make Pornography a Human-Rights Issue." *Christian Science Monitor*, 1 November 1985, 6.

A report on the Cambridge, Massachusetts, antipornography ordinance. Lindsay reviews previous unsuccessful efforts to pass such legislation, the court decisions on the Indianapolis ordinance, and the "unlikely allies and adversaries" the antipornography battle has produced.

Low, Charlotte. "Feminism Clashes With Civil Liberties Over Pornography." *Los Angeles Times*, 23 May 1984, sec. 2, 7.

In the Indianapolis antipornography ordinance, Low sees an inevitable split between feminists and "their long-time allies, the civil libertarians." She believes this was inevitable because, "Feminists view art as fundamentally a form of propaganda." She does not feel the research done on the effects of violent pornography are conclusive. Indeed, "the abstract nature of studies that are cited by the women-against-pornography movement is further evidence that the movement's aims are more propagandistic than anything else." She concludes they are "a group whose assumptions about art, fantasy and human nature defy common sense."

MacKinnon, Catharine A. "Reality, Not Fantasy." *Village Voice,*
26 March, 1985, 24.

MacKinnon responds to a number of articles ("Forbidden
Fantasy," *Village Voice,* 16 October 1984, 11–12, 16–17, 42, and
others) dealing with the antipornography legislation she coauthored
with Andrea Dworkin. She criticizes the *Voice* for errors and factual
inaccuracies. She also objects to the *Voice* alleging their support is
from the conservative right. As evidence she points out that they did
not support the Suffolk County, New York legislation where the
conservative county legislators "tried to make our bill a vehicle for
conservative values [and] had to change it substantially even to
attempt to do so." She believes their law "draws a clear line that
divides the defenders of male supremacy from those who seriously
want it ended." She is critical of *Voice* writers Nat Hentoff and
Richard Goldstein, charging, "Your lock-step liberalism sees only
risks in our initiative to empower women."

Maddocks, Melvin. " 'Snuff' and Liberal Conscience." *Christian
Science Monitor,* 1 April 1976, 30.

An essay on the protests in New York against the pornographic
movie, *Snuff.* Maddocks sees this protest as evidence "the sexual
revolution collided with the women's movement." As a result, "It has
become perceived that, if violence is a form of obscenity, obscenity
tends to be a form of violence."

Mancusi, Peter. "Free to Express—or Suppress?" *Boston Globe,*
2 June 1985, sec. A, 17.

A report on the formation of the U.S. Attorney General's
Commission on Pornography. In reference to the commission chairman, Henry Hudson, an ACLU legislature counsel says: "I don't
know much about most of the members. But I know Hudson. He
likes to be a public censor. And he does a very good job of it." The
new, unusual coalition of feminist antipornography groups and
right-wing fundamentalists is mentioned. In defense of the Minneapolis ordinance, Catharine MacKinnon says: "Censorship is an
exercise of government power to prevent the free expression of ideas.
Pornography is not ideas. It is not information." Several commission
members are questioned about its purpose.

Martin, Douglas. "Canada vs. Pornography: Even Playboy May
    Fall." *New York Times*, 3 August 1986, sec. A, 4.
    Report on legislation recently introduced in Canada that "pro-
vides for penalties of two to five years in jail for those convicted of
distributing pornography." It has the support of Fundamentalist
Christian groups and the police. It is opposed by civil libertarians.
"Even feminists, many of whom urged strong action against violent
pornography, have criticized the legislation for not discriminating
between pornography and erotica."

Math, Mara. "Andrea Dworkin Talks about Feminism and
    Pornography." *Gay Community News*, 28 December 1985–4
    January 1986, 8–9.
    In an interview with Mara Math, Andrea Dworkin tells about
her view of the antipornography movement and its importance,
comments on the ACLU's involvement with pornographers, and
gives her opinions about FACT, and why she won't debate them.
Dworkin says: "It is true that I have refused to debate FACT. The
reason is that life is short and I care a lot about how I spend my time.
I regard the women who are members of FACT as people who have
organized to hurt me and the women that I care about most, people
who have organized to stop the women who have been hurt by
pornography from getting what they deserve. . . . I take it personally.
I take it politically. I despise it, and nobody from FACT is getting a
forum on my back." Dworkin accepts the fact that there are people
who have principled reasons for being against the MacKinnon-
Dworkin ordinance. "But they commit acts of civil disobedience,
they picket, they write letters, they try to do something about the
exploitation of women by pornographers."

"Measure Seeks to Curb Violent Pornography." *New York Times*,
    10 April 1984, sec. A, 22.
    A brief Associated Press story on the antipornography ordi-
nance introduced to the Indianapolis City-County Council. Backers
of the measure say it "is intended to protect women's civil rights and
to stop violence toward women, not to stamp out eroticism or
nudity. Opponents say it constitutes censorship."

Michaelson, Judith. "Sexual Violence and the Media." *Los Angeles Times,* 8 February 1984, sec. 6, 1, 8.

Report on the symposium on Media Violence and Pornography held at the Ontario Institute for Studies in Education on 5 February. The ten-and-a-half-hour meeting, attended by more than 750 people, consisted of many panels including "educators, feminists, the U.S. Surgeon General, Toronto's only woman rabbi and an FBI official." Television shows, movies, and rock videos were all evaluated for their violent content. "A key message from the conference was that violence and pornography are linked." A feminist group, led by Andrea Dworkin, "was angered that the conference did not deal with the issues of abortion and homosexuality."

Miller, Janella. "Civil Rights, Not Censorship." *Village Voice,* 6 November 1984, 6.

Writing in response to the articles by Hentoff and Duggan in the 16 October issue of the *Village Voice* (see entries above), Miller defends the legal theory behind the MacKinnon-Dworkin ordinance. She compares the ordinance to existing libel laws and concludes "There is actually much less potential for abuse under the ordinance than there is under obscenity laws which allow judges to make moral decisions about what we should view."

"Minneapolis Asked to Attack Pornography As Rights Issue." *New York Times,* 18 December 1983, sect. A, part 1, 44.

A news report on the MacKinnon-Dworkin ordinance hearings in Minneapolis, including a concise history of how the ordinance came to be written. In response to misgivings raised by civil libertarians Ms. MacKinnon says: ". . . free speech has never been an absolute right. In this case, . . . the First Amendment guarantee must be balanced against the equal protection clause of the 14th Amendment."

"Minneapolis Mayor Vetoes Plan Defining Pornography as Sex Bias." *New York Times,* 6 January 1984, sec. A, 11.

A news article on Minneapolis Mayor Donald Fraser's veto of an amendment to the city's civil rights ordinance drafted by MacKinnon and Dworkin. Agreeing that a lot of pornographic material is degrading to women, the city council passed the ordinance by a vote of seven to six. In explaining his decision the mayor said, "I am unwilling to push onto the courts something which I believe in my own heart may express inappropriate public policy, simply because it would be expedient to do so, and rely on the courts to defend our rights."

Morgan, Robin. "Check It Out: Porn, No. But Free Speech, Yes." *New York Times,* 24 March 1978, sec. A, 27.

Morgan decries the "New Pornocracy" that is aiming for respectability and whose standard theme targets women. She believes, "Feminists may differ on strategy, but we know it is possible to be anti-pornography and pro–First Amendment." Possible alternatives for fighting pornography are zoning, educating others, picket lines, restriction on pornographic advertising, and civil disobedience, among others.

Oliver, Myrna. "Indianapolis Dispute on Porn Law Disturbs Calm of Staid, 'Clean' City." *Los Angeles Times,* 31 December 1984, sec. 1, 8.

Times staff writer, Oliver, files a lengthy report on the Indianapolis antipornography ordinance. Some people charge Indianapolis Mayor William Hudnut with playing politics with the issue. They "believe that Hudnut saw a golden opportunity to call attention to Indianapolis and at the same time strengthen his political base by joining feminists and fundamentalists, anti-pornography forces." It is not known how far the ordinance will be pursued now that Judge Barker has ruled against it. "But some council members are talking about cutting off the funding to stop what they see as unnecessary litigation of a dead issue. . . ." Although MacKinnon and Dworkin lobbied for the ordinance, "Indiana feminists sat out the whole controversy."

Orlando, Lisa. "Bad Girls and 'Good' Politics." *Village Voice Literary Supplement,* December 1982, 1, 16–19.

Orlando reviews the bitter division in the feminist movement caused by the Barnard conference, The Scholar and the Feminist IX: Towards a Politics of Sexuality. She finds one positive benefit from the bitter controversy in that the conference *Diary* (see entry for the

Diary under Alderfer in the "Books" section), which "without the confiscation and attendant publicity, might have fallen into obscurity, has been reprinted." She then reviews the *Diary of a Conference—On Sexuality,* finding it to be "amazingly dense," a tool that could be used to "remarkably enrich" the sexuality debate in the women's movement. She concludes that if the Women Against Pornography read the *Diary* "they will discover it is *not* saying that women aren't victimized, aren't oppressed, but only that concentrating on our victimization at the expense of our pleasure and power will not make us free."

Orlando, Lisa. "Lust At Last: Or Spandex Invades the Academy." *Gay Community News,* 15 May 1982, 7–10.
A description of the papers presented at the Barnard College conference, The Scholar and the Feminist IX: Towards a Politics of Sexuality. The confrontation with Women Against Pornography at the conference is reported on with some detail.

Osterman, Steven D. "The Censor's Pen Is Not Women's Best Protection; the Problem of Obscenity Cannot Be Solved by Doing Violence to the First Amendment." *Los Angeles Times,* 17 June 1984, sec. 4, 5.
Osterman is opposed to the Indianapolis antipornography ordinance because of the effect it would have on the First Amendment. "The remedy in Indianapolis must be education, not evisceration of the First Amendment." He also faults the bill for vagueness of language. "While obscenity decisions usually have viewed a work as a whole, this ordinance includes no such requirement."

Page, Sharon. "Feminists Stand Divided on Meese Commission Report." *Gay Community News,* 3–9 August 1986, 1, 11.
In reviewing feminists' reaction to the Meese Commission report Page finds: "The split in feminists ranks on reaction to the conservative-dominated report was the latest—and possibly the most dire—product of the factional schism among feminists on pornography and censorship issues." She quotes from statements by MacKinnon and Dworkin, NOW national president Eleanor Smeal, FACT, and Dorchen Leidholdt for WAP.

Page, Sharon. "Minneapolis Mayor Vetoes Anti-Porn Law." *Gay Community News*, 14 January 1984, 1–2, 7.

News report of Minneapolis Mayor Don Fraser's veto of the Minneapolis civil rights ordinance that would have declared certain kinds of pornography a violation of women's civil rights. Supporters' and nonsupporters' views are given.

Page, Sharon. "Speaking Out: 'Pimps and Porn' at Michigan." *Gay Community News*, 22 September 1984, 5.

The author of this commentary reports on a conflict at the ninth Michigan Womyn's Music Festival between those who sought cooperation and participation in a project to create feminist erotica/pornography—depending on the point of view—and those who opposed the project as just another attempt to exploit women.

Pally, Marcia. "Women in Flames." *Village Voice*, 8 May 1984, 23.

An article on Paige Mellish, organizer of Feminists Fighting Pornography, and the 8 April Women for Dignity antipornography march. Pally is somewhat skeptical of Mellish's theories. On the censorship issue Mellish says, "There already are restrictions against freedom of speech based on public safety; you can't incite a riot, for example . . . and men censor information about rape and wife abuse all the time." To which Pally adds, "Somewhere in there, two wrongs are trying to make a right." To Mellish's motto "Revolutionaries use the means they have," Pally adds: "But if we're careless about those means, what can we hope for when we arrive at the ends? What will be left after the revolution?"

Pear, Robert. "Panel Calls on Citizens to Wage National Assault on Pornography." *New York Times*, 10 July 1986, sec. A, 1, sec. B, 7.

Report on the U.S. Attorney General's Commission on Pornography's final report which suggests "concerned citizens should form 'watch groups' to file complaints, put pressure on local prosecutors, monitor judges, and if necessary, boycott merchants selling pornographic material." In accepting the report U.S. Attorney General Meese said it would not be used to foster censorship. A dissenting statement by commissioners Judith V. Becker and Ellen Levine is reviewed. Pear includes details on the establishment of the commission in February 1985 by then U.S. Attorney General William French Smith, and its methods of operation.

"Personalities." *Washington Post,* 14 February 1982, sec. D, 2.

Short news item on the announcement by Women Against Pornography of their "zap" awards for "ad campaigns that are 'demeaning to women.'" Calvin Klein was cited for his Brooke Shields ads "that consists of an above ground representation of child pornography." Maidenform was also singled out for "promoting the image of women as vacuous and passive exhibitionists."

Poggi, Stephanie. "Maine to Vote on Obscenity Law Referendum." *Gay Community News,* 14 June 1986, 1, 3, 11.

A description of the Maine obscenity referendum and a discussion of the various groups allied for and against it. Jasper Wyman of the Christian Civic League explained the lack of support from women's groups for the measure because they are "extremist radicals out of touch with feelings of women in the state. . . . They ought to be embarrassed standing up for sexism." He also mentioned a lingering bitterness over the active role he played in defeating the Equal Rights Amendment. "Activists concur that a Dworkin/MacKinnon-type of bill would have divided the feminist community, but Wyman's measure has united feminists."

"Points of View: Of Censorship." *New York Times,* 22 November 1984, sec. A, 26.

A follow-up to an editorial printed in the 19 November issue of the *New York Times* (see above: "Censors in Feminist Garb") clarifying the fact that "although the Suffolk bill is modeled on laws they [MacKinnon and Dworkin] promoted in Minneapolis and Indianapolis, they join with Women Against Pornography in opposing the New York variant." The *New York Times* reiterates its opposition to such legislation, and concludes, "The creators of this idea are right to set themselves apart from the sponsors of the Suffolk bill, but they bear some responsibility for inspiring them."

"Pornography: A Civil Rights Issue?" *Washington Post,* 4 January 1984, sec. A, 16.

This editorial strongly opposes the antipornography ordinance passed by the Minneapolis City Council. "Sensible people in Minneapolis can hardly want a law that would require judges and juries to evaluate every painting in the art gallery, every book in the library and every piece of printed material on the newsstand in terms of possible civil rights violations."

For a letter in response to this editorial see the *Washington Post*, 7 January 1984, sec. A, 16. For a reply to this letter see the *Washington Post*, 21 January 1984, sec. A, 13.

"Pornography and Civil Rights." *Los Angeles Times*, 25 March 1985, sec. 2, 4.

An editorial against the antipornography ordinance to be considered by the board of supervisors the next day. The writers agree with the feminists who oppose the measure. "Of all the social and institutional difficulties that women continue to face, pornography is not high on the list. Many people may not like it, but the danger that pornography presents is exaggerated." They suggest the ordinance should be "withdrawn and forgotten."

"Protestors Press Pornography Law: 20 Are Arrested in Minneapolis in Bid Against City Council Delay On an Ordinance." *New York Times*, 14 July 1984, 8, 46.

United Press International report on the arrest of twenty antipornography protesters after they rushed the platform in the Minneapolis City Council chamber. They were angry over the council's vote to delay consideration of an antipornography ordinance if the mayor vetoed it. The mayor and a council member are both quoted as saying further action should await a decision in the Indianapolis case.

"Putting Porno In Its Place." *Wall Street Journal*, 28 February 1986, 24, eastern ed.

Editorial on the Supreme Court's decision on the Indianapolis antipornography ordinance and local zoning regulations regarding pornography. "The content of pornography will keep being protected. By contrast, the places where pornography can be shown will be substantially restricted."

Rather, John. "Pornography Bill Stirs Furor in Suffolk." *New York Times,* 7 October 1984, section 11LI, 1.

A report on a hearing in Suffolk County, New York, on an antipornography bill sponsored by legislator Michael D'Andre. In defense of the bill D'Andre says: "I can't see how anyone can think all this violence and pornography is what's meant by the First Amendment." Speaking at the hearing, Lisa Duggin, a member of FACT, said: "This law doesn't do anything to stop real violence and pain in women's lives." Also at the hearing Bill Baird, who runs two birth control centers on Long Island, read passages from the Bible that seemed to fit the bill's criteria for objectionable pornography. This so enraged conservative legislator, Rose Caracappa, "that she advanced on Mr. Baird outside the hearing room and raised her hand to deliver a blow. . . ."

Rich, B. Ruby. "Anti-Porn: Soft Issue, Hard World." *Village Voice,* 20 July 1982, 1, 16–18, 30.

An essay and analysis of the current antipornography movement developed around a review of the film *Not A Love Story.* The author says the film is "concerned, engaged, up-to-the-minute on social questions, but slick, manipulative, avoiding all the hard questions." Rich refers to the antipornography movement as "displacement" and "confusion" and says that pornography needs to be studied, not ignored or suppressed.

See also a response in the *Village Voice,* 17 August 1982, 27.

Rubin, Gayle. "Anti-Porn Laws and Women's Liberation." *Gay Community News,* 22 December 1984, 8–9.

Rubin deplores censorship and repression of materials in the feminist community and points out its dangers to women when applied to material the Moral Majority does not like. "The growing consensus between the women's movement and the right wing on pornography is a grave threat to our freedom."

Russ, Joanna. "Pornography and Sexuality Debates: Examining the History." *Gay Community News,* 7–13 September 1986, 5.

Russ says that the reaction of feminists and others to the Meese Commission report has "frozen into one of two positions: either sexual pleasure is an inexplicable, uncaused absolute and absolutely OK or anything else takes precedence and sexual pleasure is (almost by definition) patriarchally corrupt." Russ says that the split is no accident and is a result of the so-called "sex reform movement" of the 1890s to 1920s. "The fathers of the movement, like Ernest van der Velde and Havelock Ellis (it had no mothers) were reacting against feminism of the 1880s and 1890s. One of the prominent features of European feminism of the time (it ended not with the vote but with the political witch hunts of World War I) was women's anger at male exploitation." So men invented the sex reform movement. Russ goes on to document the similarity between what these men said about liberated sexuality and what is said by the "pro-sex" and the anti-pornography factions today. Russ points out that the historic connections are important to know if the issues are to be dealt with correctly. She sees "The real issues surrounding the phenomena like the anti-pornography movement are issues of power, exploitation, and the extent to which all of us have been affected by the economic-political-social system we live in."

"SJC Orders Cambridge to Put Antiporn Referendum on Ballot."
    Boston Globe, 3 October 1985, 18.
    A brief report on the state Supreme Judicial Court ruling in favor of the Women's Alliance Against Pornography's appeal to overrule the Cambridge City Council. The antipornography referendum question will appear on the November ballot.

Savage, David G. "Violence and Women: Researchers Condemn
    R-Rated Films as Worse Offenders Than Pornographic
    Movies." *Los Angeles Times*, 1 June 1985, sec. 2, 1, 6.
    The report of a symposium held at the annual meeting of the American Association for the Advancement of Science. Edward Donnerstein reported, "It is the 'violent message or violent scenes, not the sexual explicit material' that is the real concern. We've found no effects for sexual content alone." Joseph Scott of Ohio State University, compared the number of violent scenes in R, G, PG, and X-rated movies. "No matter how we looked at it or what measure of violence we used, the X-rated movies had the least violence of any type of movie," Scott said. In response to the social scientists, Catharine MacKinnon, a University of California at Los Angeles

visiting law professor and author of the antipornography statute pending in Los Angeles, said, "The distinction between sex and violence is a false one."

See, Carolyn. "Angry Women and Brutal Men." *New York Times
    Book Review,* 28 December 1980, 4, 14.
    A review of *Take Back the Night,* edited by Laura Lederer (New York: William Morrow, 1980), and *Women, Sex and Pornography* (New York: Macmillan, 1980) by Beatrice Faust. The reviewer summarizes the thirty-two articles in the Lederer book as saying that pornography has as its sole reason for being, the debasement of women. "These women are more than just a little hot under the collar." She says that Beatrice Faust in her book "really does talk—courageously—about sex and pornography and about how women's ideas about them differ from men's." She finds Ms. Faust unthreatening but not *Take Back the Night.*
    For readers' responses to this review see "Letters," *New York Times,* 25 January, 1981, sec. 7, 29.

Serrin, William. "Sex Is a Multibillion Business in U.S. and
    Expanding." *New York Times,* 9 February 1981, sec. B, 1.
    "Opponents of Flourishing Sex Industry Hindered by Its
    Open Public Acceptance." *New York Times,* 10 February 1981,
    sec. B, 6.
    A two-part series on the growth of the pornography industry in the United States, both in dollars, explicitness of content, and general acceptance. "Sex items that prosecutors a few years ago would have zealously sought to proscribe now escape scrutiny." One of the problems for groups trying to fight pornography is an "inability to agree on what it is they are fighting." An example included is of a man who went to the Women Against Pornography office to seek their help in banning a homosexual statue in Christopher Park, only to find the people there were in favor of it. Police action, or lack of it, against pornography and the sex industry are also discussed.

Shannon, William V. "The Pornography Evil." *Boston Globe,* 24 July
    1985, 15.
    Shannon writes of the proliferation of pornography which "contributes to a further erosion of the moral values on which

civilization depends." He sees the Indianapolis antipornography ordinance as a "promising new approach" to the problem. In rebuttal to the claims that the ordinance is broad enough to include *The Taming of the Shrew,* he responds: "The risk that a judge somewhere might mistake Shakespeare for pornography is far smaller than the very real damage that 'adult' books and films are doing."

Shenon, Philip. "Justice Dept. Pornography Study Finds Material is Tied to Violence." *New York Times,* 14 May 1986, sec. A, 17.

Shenon reports on release of the introduction to the Meese Commission's final report and its list of recommendations. The commission said, "Most pornography in the United States would be classified as 'degrading,' particularly to women." The article lists seven of the specific recommendations of the commission. Shenon contrasts the conclusions of the Meese Commission with those of the 1970 presidential commission.

Shenon, Philip. "Meese Named Panel to Study How to Control Pornography." *New York Times,* 21 May 1985, sec. A, 21.

A news article on the formation of the Justice Department Commission on Pornography. The panel will be headed by Henry E. Hudson, a prosecutor from Arlington County, Virginia who has banished most pornography from his county. A spokesman for the American Civil Liberties Union said, in regard to the commission: "I'm afraid there is a train marked 'censorship' which has just left the station." The other ten members of the commission are also named.

For a similar article see Tofani, Loretta, "Meese Names Pornography Panel," *Washington Post,* 21 May 1985, sec. A, 16.

Sherman, Laurie. "Symposium Illuminates Porn Debate." *Gay Community News,* 19 October 1985, 3, 10, 11.

A report of the symposium organized before the Cambridge vote on the MacKinnon-Dworkin antipornography ordinance. It became a debate over the ordinance rather than a conference on broader issues as envisioned by the planners (several women's organizations at Harvard and MIT). Speakers are reported on and their arguments presented. FACT members reported being disinvited to present their views.

Shipp, E. R. "Civil Rights Law Against Pornography Is
Challenged." *New York Times,* 15 May 1984, sec. A, 14.

News article on the Indianapolis antipornography ordinance,
signed by Mayor Hudnut on 1 May. Bookstores, trade associations,
and a cable television station immediately challenged the law. The
director of the Indiana Civil Liberties Union "charges it will create 'a
cultural wasteland.'" Beulah Coughenour, the law's sponsor, is
philosophical about its establishment as law. "You have to start
somewhere. If for some reason the court finds the ordinance flawed
and sends it back on technical grounds, but says the concept is still
valid, then we'll know better how to try it again."

Shipp, E. R. "A Feminist Offensive Against Exploitation." *New
York Times,* 10 June 1984, sec. D, 2.

News article describing the unusual coalitions that have formed
in Minneapolis and Indianapolis in support of the MacKinnon-
Dworkin antipornography ordinances. Includes the current status of
the laws: Minneapolis ordinance vetoed by the mayor, but supporters are urging that it be passed again. Indianapolis passed the
ordinance, the mayor signed it, and an hour later a lawsuit was filed
against it. A hearing is scheduled for 30 July.

Shipp, E. R. "Federal Judge Hears Arguments on Validity of
Indianapolis Pornography Measure." *New York Times,* 31 July
1984, sec. A, 10.

A news report on the hearing before Federal District Judge
Sarah Barker on the Indianapolis antipornography ordinance. A
lawyer for the city's legal department argued that "pornography is
not and should not be protected by the Constitution." Michael
Bamberger, lawyer for Media Coalition Inc., argued that "pornographic depictions of women, as hateful as they may be to our
society in general, nevertheless have a right to be expressed."

Sitomer, Curtis J. "Censorship, the Spirit and the Letter." *Christian
Science Monitor,* 3 August 1984, sec. B, 6, national ed.

An essay against the Indianapolis antipornography ordinance.
Sitomer agrees the time may be ripe for a new "war on porn" given
the expanding forms, such as video cassettes and phone services,

through which it is available. "The question now is: Are we going to face up to a serious societal problem in a rational and lawful way, or will we let emotional outrage trigger action that could bring about Constitution-defying, broad-based censorship?"

Sitomer, Curtis J. "A Nationwide Boycott of Pornography Might Do What the Courts Can't." *Christian Science Monitor,* 12 January 1984, 19, national ed.

As the title of the article reveals, Sitomer suggests a nationwide boycott of "obscene books, films, and sexual paraphernalia." He reviews various court battles to fight pornography and the Minneapolis ordinance. As these methods are being tested and worked out a boycott could begin. "A boycott against obscene stuff isn't merely within our legal rights—it's a moral responsibility."

Sitomer, Curtis J. "Panel Sees Porn as Civil Rights Issue." *Christian Science Monitor,* 14 May 1986, 1, 6, 7, national ed.

A report that the forthcoming report from the Attorney General's Commission on Pornography will " 'endorse the concepts of the civil rights approach' to curbing pornography." Reviews the judicial history of the Indianapolis ordinance, and varying opinions on the anticipated report.

Sitomer, Curtis J. "Sifting Out Pornography From Free Speech." *Christian Science Monitor,* 11 July 1985, 21, national ed.

A survey of the current antipornography efforts, including the antipornography/civil rights of women ordinances in Indianapolis, Los Angeles, and Minneapolis, the Attorney General's Commission on Pornography, and the recently passed New York bill that forbids the display of sexually explicit materials in stores open to the general public.

Stevenson, Gail. "Tolerance of Porn Traumatizes Women." *Los Angeles Times,* 28 May 1985, sec. 2, 5.

Stevenson, a clinical psychologist, believes pornography is more problematic for women today because they have an increased sense of worth, that makes "pornographic humiliation" less tolerable, and because "pornography has become more violent and more pervasive in our society." She finds a common reaction to pornography is rage, which is often internalized, and this leads to depression. "Another clinical reaction to exposure to pornography is sexual dysfunction." She believes "we must build socially sanctioned mechanisms through which women may effectively respond to pornography," such as the ordinances before the Los Angeles County Board of Supervisors and City Council.

"The Story of X." *New York Times,* 13 July 1986, sec. E, 28.

This editorial characterizes the final report of the Meese Commission as a "well-meant, windy muddle." The writer concedes the report contains a realistic discussion of child pornography. In an effort to present a unified report from the whole commission, however, "it ends up reasonable in tone but opaque in content."

"Suffolk Officials Vote Down Bill on Pornography." *New York Times,* 27 December 1984, sec. B, 5.

Suffolk County legislators voted down a tough antipornography bill by a vote of nine to eight. Michael D'Andre, the sponsor of the bill, "said he would seek support to recall the bill for another vote." Several of those voting against it believed it was unconstitutional. The country attorney said it violated the state constitution "and usurped powers of the state legislature."

Suplee, Curt, and James Lardner. "Writers of the World, Unite!: Congress of Authors Assaults 'Literary Industrial Complex.' " *Washington Post,* 12 October 1981, sec. D, 1, 3.

A report on the American Writers' Conference held in New York City. A panel session on Eros, Language, and Pornography "developed into a verbal brawl between feminists." Andrea Dworkin led the faction urging women to organize against pornography. Journalist Ellen Willis countered that women are demeaned just as much by gothic novels and romances. "Opposition to pornography is opposition to letting women expand their sexual freedom," said Willis.

Taylor, Stuart, Jr. "High Court Backs Use of Zoning to Regulate Showing of Sex Films." *New York Times,* 26 February 1986, sec. A, 1, 20.

A report on the Supreme Court ruling on 25 January "that local zoning officials have broad powers to restrict the location of movie theaters showing sexually explicit films." The ruling comes a day after the Court struck down the Indianapolis antipornography ordinance. "Today's ruling is consistent with that decision, but it also reaffirms that the Court affords sexually explicit materials less protection than other kinds of speech, especially political speech."

Taylor, Stuart, Jr. "Pornography Foes Lose New Weapon in
    Supreme Court." *New York Times*, 25 February 1986,
    sec. A, 1, 26.
    News report on the Supreme Court six-to-three decision upholding the ruling of the Federal Appeals Court that the Indianapolis antipornography ordinance violates the First Amendment right of free speech. The decision was issued without an opinion. "Chief Justice Warren E. Burger and Associate Justices William H. Rehnquist and Sandra Day O'Connor dissented from the summary treatment of the case saying it should be set down for detailed briefing and oral argument." The "summary affirmance" by the Supreme Court "establishes a precedent binding on all courts." Indianapolis city officials "argued that the Indianapolis ordinance was an 'innovative and promising' way to help women, children and other victims of the pornography industry."

Terp, Christine. "Women Against Pornography." *Christian Science
    Monitor*, 2 October 1979, sec. B, 8, national ed.
    Terp reports on the six-month-old New York organization Women Against Pornography, and the conference it sponsored attended by over 750 women. "What feminists are particularly concerned about is the brutal direction pornography has taken in the last few years, with writing and film concentrating more and more on physical violence." The research of Donnerstein is discussed, as well as pornography's influence on advertising, album covers, and fashion magazines. Various civil disobedience tactics to combat the sale of pornography are discussed. Susan Brownmiller, a founding member of WAP, believes what needs to be changed is "men's distorted notions of sexuality."

"U.S. Court Rejects an Anti-Smut Law." *New York Times*,
    28 August 1985, sec. A, 21.
    The Associated Press report on the U.S. Court of Appeals for the Seventh Circuit ruling that the Indianapolis ordinance defining

pornography as a violation of women's civil rights is unconstitutional. In the opinion of the court, panel Judge George Easterbrook wrote: "The state may not ordain preferred viewpoints in this way. The Constitution forbids the state to declare one perspective right and silence opponents." The defendants have not made a decision about a further appeal.

A similar article appeared in the *Washington Post*, 28 August 1985, sec. A, 16, under the title, "Pornography Law Overturned."

Vance, Carole S. "Meese Commission: The Porn Police Attack." *Gay Community News*, 27 July–2 August 1986, 3, 6, 12.

Vance finds that the Meese Commission report "endorses a conservative agenda which is deeply committed to obscenity law as the means to control sexually explicit materials." She reviews the appointment of the commissioners, seven of whom had already publically stated their opposition to pornography. She goes on to detail criticisms of the commission's operation such as the narrow topics of its hearings and the uneven treatment of witnesses. She questions the undefined use of language in the commission report: "Multipurpose terms like 'degrading' can appeal to conservative and moderate audiences, while loaded terms like 'violent' pornography invite automatic and uncritical judgments about sexual material." Vance believes use of such terms by prosecutors, judges and juries can have serious repercussions for gay and lesbian images.

Vollmer, Ted. "Counsel Urges Compromise in Pornography Law." *Los Angeles Times*, 4 June 1985, sec. 2, 1, 6.

A report on Los Angeles County Counsel DeWitt Clinton's proposed change in the antipornography ordinance before the County Board of Supervisors. Clinton proposed that the county "allow people to seek civil damages from producers of pornography only if they can demonstrate that they were coerced into making or viewing materials depicting sexual violence or sexual abuse." He put forth his compromise when the County Commission for Women refused to alter their original antipornography proposal. Karen Davis, a member of Women Against Pornography, said of Clinton's proposal: "I wouldn't call it compromise language, I would call it window dressing." Clinton also suggested the county adopt the U.S. Supreme Court's definition of obscenity.

Vollmer, Ted. "County Rejects Wide Anti-Smut Law; 2 Weaker
Ones OKd." *Los Angeles Times*, 5 June 1985, sec. 2, 1, 6.

A report on the Los Angeles County Board of Supervisors
adoption of compromise ordinances instead of the antipornography
measure proposed by the County Commission for Women. The
measures that passed "would permit anyone forced to participate in
making or viewing materials that depict sexual violence or abuse to
sue those responsible for making the material" and "would also allow
assault victims to recover monetary damages from pornographers if
the victims could show that they had been assaulted because their
attackers had viewed pornographic materials." At a hearing before
the final vote, Betty Rosenstein defended the Commission for
Women's ordinance, saying: "The harm in pornography far out-
weighs any problems, any risks." Feminist attorney Gloria Allred
said the county's "reluctance to adopt such an ordinance is a 'slap in
the face of women.' "

Wald, Matthew L. "Maine Anti-Obscenity Plan Soundly Defeated."
New York Times, 12 June 1986, sec. A, 27.

The Maine referendum on obscene material was defeated "by a
margin of more than two to one." Mary Lou Dyer of the Maine Civil
Liberties Union said the vote showed " 'Maine women understand
that the problems of abused women and children lie much deeper
than porn.' "

Wald, Matthew L. "Obscenity Debate Focuses Attention on Maine,
Where Voters Weigh Issue." *New York Times*, 10 June 1986,
sec. A, 18.

Report on the proposed Maine referendum on obscenity to be
voted on this week. It requires prison terms "for those who sell,
promote or 'give for value' materials that are found to be obscene." It
relies on the 1973 Supreme Court case, *Miller vs. California*, for the
definition of obscenity. Supporters of the measure include the
Roman Catholic Bishop of Maine, Concerned Citizens for Decency,
and conservative, evangelical Christians. The referendum is opposed
by "librarians, feminists and civil libertarians." They believe it would
"lead to purges in libraries, banning of sex education texts and
perhaps other limitations on what citizens can read and see."

Wehrwein, Austin C. "Mayor Vetoes Ordinance in Minneapolis
    Labeling Pornography Sex Bias." *Washington Post,* 6 January
    1984, sec. A, 2.
    Report on Minneapolis Mayor Donald Fraser's veto of the city
ordinance amendment regarding pornography. Fraser said: "The
remedy sought through the ordinance as drafted is neither appropri-
ate nor enforceable within our cherished tradition and constitutionally protected right of free speech." He also rejected the theory that
pornography necessarily leads directly to violence against women.
Catharine MacKinnon, reacting to the veto, said "she disagreed with
Fraser because she was sure that the data showed a causal effect
between pornography and violence against women, and in any
event, the First Amendment has never been absolute."

Wehrwein, Austin C. "Smut Is Declared Illegal Sex Bias In
    Minneapolis." *Washington Post,* 31 December 1983, sec. A, 3.
    Report on the 30 December passage by the Minneapolis City
Council of an antipornography ordinance in a seven-to-six vote.
"The measure gathered momentum because of a general increase in
rape cases here, including two particularly brutal ones in the past
two months." The ordinance was written by MacKinnon and
Dworkin, who "hoped to force a speedy test of both workability and
constitutionality of the amendment by urging the council to make
pornography—as they define it—a form of discrimination under the
14th Amendment." Gives background on the effort to pass the
ordinance, and who supported it.

Weil, Martin, and Peter Eng. "Women March Against
    Pornography." *Washington Post,* 27 September 1981, sec. B, 8.
    A news report of a "Take Back the Night" march held the
previous evening. The demonstration by about 450 people was
sponsored by a coalition of groups "including the Washington Area
Women's Center, the Rape Crisis Center, D.C. Feminists Against
Pornography, and My Sister's Place, a women's shelter." It came at
the "close of a week of antirape seminars and workshops."

Will, George F. " 'Rights' vs. Smut in Minneapolis." *Washington
    Post,* 8 January 1984, sec. C, 7.
    Will believes the vote of the Minneapolis City Council on the
antipornography amendment showed "how awkward are attempts

to act wisely on unwise premises." He finds the assertions in the amendment "are over-reaching, a tactic of desperation." Yet he understands the need for such desperation given the current liberal interpretation of the First Amendment. "If women can find more convincing language to use when pressing the point they made in Minneapolis, and I wish them well, they will alter community standards and thereby perhaps expand the power of local authorities to regulate pornography."

For letters in response to this article see the *Post* for 13 January sec. A, 13.

Willis, Ellen. "Nature's Revenge." *The New York Times Book Review*, 12 July 1981, sec. 7, 9.

Ellis describes the irony of feminist outrage at pornography matching that of the New Right. "This peculiar confluence raises the question of whether the current feminist preoccupation with pornography is an attempt to extend the movements' critique of sexism or whether it is evidence that feminists have been affected by the conservative climate and are unconsciously moving with the cultural tide." Ellis then reviews Susan Griffin's *Pornography and Silence* and Andrea Dworkin's *Pornography* and says that "these two very different books suggest that it is both." (For annotation and complete citation, see "Books" section).

For a response to this review, see Dorchen Leidholdt in "Letters," *New York Times Book Review*, 23 August 1981, 3.

Willis, Ellen. "Who is a Feminist?: A Letter to Robin Morgan." *Village Voice Literary Supplement*, December 1982, 16–17.

Willis writes in response to charges by Morgan in her book, *The Anatomy of Freedom* (Garden City, N.Y.: Anchor Press, 1982) that she and four others are "enemies of women and feminism" and that Willis "has on various occasions championed pornography." Willis cites the activities of all of the accused individuals in the women's movement and their publications and concludes, "If they cannot call themselves feminists who can? And again, who are you to decide?" On the question of pornography, Willis replies: "Where we differ is that I do not think *all* pornography can simply be condemned out of hand, nor do I think there is any objective way to distinguish between 'pornography' and 'erotica,' nor do I think equating pornography (words or images) with violence (acts) makes logical sense." Finally, Willis regrets Morgan's attack because it signals a rigidity within the women's movement that could be very damaging. "A commitment to diversity, free inquiry, the constant questioning of received ideas (including our own) must be the governing principle of a radical movement; otherwise feminism is merely another lifeless, dogmatic, authoritarian sect."

Yardley, Jonathan. "The Porn Predicament: It's Not Being Prudish To Want To Stop the Sleaze." *Washington Post,* 9 January 1984, sec. B, 1.

Yardly believes the sexual revolution that began in the 1960s, has, as revolution has a way of doing, gone too far. As a result " 'Last Tango in Paris' and 'Deep Throat' gave way to snuff flicks and kiddie porn." He sees the antipornography ordinance passed in Minneapolis as a well-needed reaction to the excesses of pornography. "The statute was a piece of doctrine feminist mischief, but the sentiments that helped it win passage cannot be taken lightly. Not the feminist one—the notion that pornography somehow 'discriminates' against women is a gross oversimplification and distortion of a very complex reality—but the widely held belief among ordinary citizens that the erotic revolution has gotten out of hand."

4.
Nonprint Media

This section includes listings of films, slideshows, video recordings, and other audiovisual media on women and pornography. All but one of these presentations were produced in the 1980s. All annotations are prepared from secondary sources except for *The Porning of America*, the slide show prepared by Women Against Pornography, and *Not a Love Story*.

"Commentary (MA Gang Rape Trial)" [television broadcast]. Bill Moyers reporting. 30 March 1984, 5:50 p.m. CBS.

Moyers's commentary is on the New Bedford, Massachusetts, defense attorneys' efforts to portray the gang rape victim as the villain in the trial of her attackers. The psychological process known as "rape myth" is explained. A University of Wisconsin study pertinent to the issue is discussed. The relationship between pornography and tolerance of violence against women is considered.

Gilboa, Netta. *When the Whip Comes Down: 300 Abusive Images of Women in the Media* [photographic slides]. Illinois Sociological Association, 1983.

A slide presentation combining 300 images from record album covers, department store windows, advertisements, and both soft- and hard-core pornography illustrates how such themes as rape, spouse abuse, child pornography, incest, lesbianism, and torture are glorified and trivialized by the mass media. Explored are censorship issues, backlash on the feminist movement, positive portrayals of women, and strategies for change. These materials have been shown to over 350 audiences across the United States, prisons, churches, high schools, colleges, women's groups, and conferences.

"Indianapolis, In/Pornography Law" [television broadcast]. Meredith Vieria reporting. 30 July 1984, 5:30 p.m. CBS.

A controversial antipornography law here is examined. Attorney Catharine MacKinnon, who doesn't consider promoting abuse of women entertainment, explains the purpose of the law. Arguments for and against the ordinance are summarized. An Indiana Civil Liberties Union spokesperson and a videotape dealer also comment on the ordinance.

Killing Us Softly: Advertising Images of Women [motion picture].
Created by Jean Kilbourne. Cambridge, Mass.: Cambridge Documentary Films, 1985. Running time: 30 minutes, 16mm.
This half-hour film is based upon a multimedia presentation created by Jean Kilbourne. Its focus is on how the $50-billion advertising industry exploits images of women and of sexuality to peddle products to the American consumer. It is included here because it raises the issue of glorification of violence against women in advertising. This kind of advertising was a target of early antipornography activists.

"Minneapolis/Pornography Law" [television broadcast]. Derrick Blakely reporting. 30 December 1983, 5:40 p.m. CBS.
A report on passage of the antipornography ordinance. Andrea Dworkin explains the law. Catharine MacKinnon notes the basic issue at stake. Opposition to the law is outlined.

"Minneapolis/Pornography" [television broadcast]. Cassandra Clayton reporting. 30 December 1983, 5:42 p.m. NBC.
A report from Minneapolis on the passage of the antipornography ordinance. The law's definition of pornography and criticism of its vagueness are noted. City Council member, Barbara Carolson, and Minnesota Civil Liberties Union spokesman, Matthew Stark, are interviewed.

"Minneapolis/Pornography Law" [television broadcast]. Dan Rather reporting. 5 January 1984, 5:47 p.m. CBS.
A studio report on Minneapolis Mayor Don Fraser's veto of the antipornography law based on sex discrimination. Details given.

"Minneapolis/Pornography Ordinance" [television broadcast]. Tom Brokaw reporting. 5 January 1984, 5:45 p.m. NBC.
A studio report on Minneapolis mayor's veto of the antipornography ordinance. Details given.

"Minneapolis/Pornography Ordinance" [television broadcast].
    Peter Jennings reporting. 5 January 1984, 6:24 p.m. ABC.
    A studio report on Minneapolis Mayor Don Fraser's veto of the
    antipornography ordinance. Details given.

Not a Love Story [motion picture]. Directed by Bonnie Sherr Klein
    with the participation of Linda Lee Tracy. National Film
    Board of Canada (Studio D), 1982. Running time: 75
    minutes. 35mm.
    A documentary on pornography and its impact on women. *Not
    a Love Story* is a record of former stripper, Linda Lee Tracey, and her
    coming to terms with "her profession, her milieu, and herself"
    (Vincent Canby, *New York Times,* 11 June 1982, sec. C, 18). The
    film is also a consideration of pornography and feminism as reflected
    in filmed interviews with feminists such as Kate Millet, Margaret
    Atwood, and people who work in the porn trade.

"The Porning of America" [television broadcast]. 2 January 1986.
    National Educational Television.
    The question posed to a panel by moderator Marty Goldsen-
    sohn was: "Explicit sex—is it new freedom, or is it ruining America?"
    Panelists were Kate Ellis, Rutgers University professor; Richard E.
    McLawhorn, National Coalition Against Pornography; Debbie
    Lindner; and Betty Friedan. Viewpoints were given by Al Goldstein,
    editor of *Screw;* Marcia Pally, FACT; Dr. Robert Abramovitz; and
    Valerie Heller of Women Against Pornography. A married couple
    who rent pornographic videos for home use also offered a point of
    view. The moderator pointed out that pornography has always been
    available but never so openly before. To sum up the points of view:
    the couple thought pornographic videos helped their sex life and
    were fun; Debbie Lindner doesn't like kids to see the negative
    portrayal of women; the psychiatrist, Dr. Abramovitz is concerned
    about the effect of media on children and believes they see it as
    "mainstream behavior," not fantasy; and, Marcia Pally thinks its OK
    for children to see sex. Pally believes we ought to find out why "S
    and M is so hot." She believes it has to do with the status of power in
    our society. Richard McLawhorn believes that there is more than
    enough evidence, that there is a connection between violence de-
    picted and violence acted out. Kate Ellis sees the suppression of

pornography as the suppression of women and their new-found sexuality. Betty Freidan wants the women's movement to drop the whole subject and fight the important battles—abortion rights, the feminization of poverty, and reactionary politics.

Pornography: A Feminist Legal Response [sound recording]. New
   York: National Conference on Women and Law, 1985,
   cassette.
   A transcript of a workshop on pornography which took place at the Sixteenth National Conference on Women and Law in New York City, 24 March 1985. Some of the speakers suggested that existing laws and legal doctrine are sufficient to respond to the victimization of anyone from pornography. Ruth Colker and others responded that although this may be true in theory, the courts have failed to apply this existing legal protection.

"Pornography Protest" [television broadcast]. Bob Schieffer
   reporting. 30 October 1979, 6:45 p.m. CBS.
   A studio report on the antipornography protest in New York City sponsored by Women Against Pornography. Tape shown.

"Pornography/Sex Discrimination/Minneapolis" [television
   broadcast]. Jerry King reporting. 30 December 1983, 6:13
   p.m. ABC.
   The antipornography ordinance and its implications are explained. ACLU spokesperson, Linda Ojala, feels the ordinance is unconstitutional. Catharine MacKinnon feels pornography is a practice of subordination of sexually exploited women. Mayor Don Fraser believes the law faces serious problems.

Rate It X [motion picture]. Directed by Lucy Winer and Paula
   DeKoenigsberg; based on a concept by Claudette
   Charbonneau. OTM Production, New York. N.Y., 1985.
   Running time: 95 minutes, 16mm and 35mm.
   This is a documentary selection of about twenty scenes showing American males "exercising their machismo." Alternatively funny and outrageous, these men collectively personify male-dominated American society from the cradle to the grave, literally—as men in the film talk about inculcating masculine values into the man-child

(no dolls!), and shopping for caskets (for men, heavy oak; for women, silk ruffles and floral designs)" (*Variety*, 28 August 1985). There is an interview with a producer of "S/M horror films." The chief cartoonist of *Hustler* justifies his "Chester the Molester" series about a "goofy, but laughable psychopathic rapist." The editor of *Players* says nude centerfolds of black women foster black pride. There is a tour of Show World, the largest sex emporium "in the world."

Sex Roles for Sale: Sex Stereotyping in the Media [photographic
    slides]. New York: Women Against Pornography, 1983.
    A slide show for teenagers. It contains forty-four slides, cassette, lesson plan, and bibliography: both violent and positive sex role imagery are depicted.

Women, Pornography, and the First Amendment [sound recording].
    Catharine MacKinnonn, speaker. Boulder: American Civil
    Liberties Union, 1985, cassette 5.
    In defense of her model antipornography ordinance, MacKinnon says "pornographers are the practitioners of a ruling ideology of misogyny, racism and sexualized bigotry." Her opponent in the debate warns against a coalition of feminists and right-wingers and the "diversion of women from more important issues." This took place at the 1985 ACLU biennial conference in Boulder, Colorado.

5.
Unpublished Material

The items in this section are, for the most part, papers prepared for presentation at academic association conferences. One item is an article prepared for publication. Another is documentation presented by Joseph Burton, of Playboy Enterprises, at one of the U.S. Attorney General's Commission on Pornography hearings.

Brigman, William E. "Pornography as Political Expression: The Supreme Court, Sexual Censorship and the 'Decent Society' Argument." Paper presented at the Southwest Social Science Association, 25–28 March 1981, Dallas, Texas.

The author from the University of Missouri–St. Louis, challenges the "distorted, logical and aesthetic bases of the two-level theory of communication—a theory of communication adopted by Supreme Court Justice Brennan—which excluded obscenity from First Amendment protection on the grounds that it didn't express any ideas." Brigman provides a history of the development of the law of obscenity and then sets out to prove that pornography has ideational content, expresses a philosophical viewpoint, and is a form of political experience, all of which gives it protection under the First Amendment. Statements of feminists in the antipornography movement are quoted to support his thesis.

Burton, Doris-Jean. "Feminism, Pornography, and Public Opinion." Paper presented at the 1985 Southern Political Science Association Convention, 7–9 November 1985, Nashville, Tennessee.

Burton describes the factors which have resulted in recent attention being paid to pornography: it is more readily available; readily available pornography has an increased emphasis on the combination of sex and violence; and new research on the effects of pornography indicate that not all pornography is harmless. The paper examines the current state of public opinion on pornography; analyzes that opinion, not only by sex but among females with respect to working women and housewives; examines change in opinion over the last decade; explores the relationship of attitudes

toward the regulation of pornography to attitudes toward women's
role in society and attitudes toward sexual behavior; and, finally, the
paper probes whether feminist efforts to change public opinion and
public policy are likely to be effective by examining the chracteristics
of those who argue or disagree with feminists about pornography
and its regulation.

Burton, Joseph. "Contemporary Research Between 1970–1985
    Relating to Exposure to Explicit Material and Aggression or
    Antisocial Consequences." Documentation presented by Mr.
    Burton for Playboy Enterprises, at a hearing of the U.S.
    Attorney General's Commission on Pornography, 1985.
    This document is part of Burton's testimony before U.S. Attor-
ney General Meese's Commission on Pornography and consists of a
statement that reflects his testimony plus a summary of research
between 1970 through 1985 relating to the "alleged causal relationship between explicit sexual material and anti-social conduct." His
statement deals with obscenity cases, First Amendment issues, and
whether or not pornography is dangerous. Burton says he is not
only an advocate of the First Amendment but also a "spokesman for
a frequent target of censorship efforts—*Playboy Magazine.*" There are
sixty-three pages of research articles on pornography, with summaries. A separate list of all publications included concludes this report.

Colker, Ruth. "Published Consentless Sexual Portrayals: A
    Proposed Framework for Analysis." 1985. Typescript.
    The author, a law professor at Tulane University, includes some
discussion of law and the antipornography movement. The MacKinnon-Dworkin model ordinance is printed. This unpublished article
is especially useful for its copius references, in footnotes, to law cases,
and articles in law reviews and journals.

Gray, Susan H. "Pornography and Violence Against Women: Is
    There Hard Evidence on Hard-Core?" Eastern Sociological
    Society, 1981.
    The current controversy over the effects of pornography on
treatment of, and underlying attitudes toward, women is examined.
Empirical work, done in an attempt to sort out issues raised since the
report of the President's Commission on Obscenity and Pornogra-

phy, is reviewed. There appears to be little evidence for a relationship between exposure to hard-core pornography and aggressive behavior in males. However, levels of aggression are generally increased by highly erotic materials. The subtleties of the recent body of literature on the effects of pornography and the implications of current research for "normal" male treatment of women are discussed.

Stock, Wendy. "Women's Affective Responses and Subjective Reactions to Exposure to Violent Pornography." Paper presented at the Conference of the Association of Women in Psychology, 8 March 1985, New York, New York.

In the words of the author: "This study investigated the effects of violent pornography on women, considering both subjective and genital sexual arousal. The design permitted comparison of the effects of pre-exposure to various audiotaped versions of erotic stimuli (some involving rape) on female subjects who were all subsequently exposed to a realistic depiction of rape." The methodology of the study is detailed and the author concludes from the finding "that women are not aroused and do not feel positively toward realistic depictions of rape which describe victim suffering." Dr. Stock is a member of the Department of Psychology at Texas A & M University.

Warshay, Diana Wortman, and Leon H. Warshay. "Covert Violence Against Women." North Central Sociological Association, 1978.

Examined are some of the subtle, often unlabeled means, methods, techniques, or devices through which men control women. These means, linguistic and nonverbal, intimidate and subjugate women, reinforcing the superiority of men. The various means used are considered to be forms of covert violence in that they cause injury (in the broadest sense) and carry the potential of physical force. Among linguistic and paralinguistic methods on the institutional level that do violence to women are: the use of "man" to stand for all people, the quantity and variety of obscene terms in the language that derogate women, the content of pornography, and the many decisions about women's bodies and lives made by male legislators.

6.
Organizations

The listing of organizations includes contact information for those who want to join one of the groups or be added to a mailing list. Groups listed are here because they responded to a request for information. Information was up-to-date at the time of publication. However, these groups do change their locations from time to time.

ACWIT (A Community Is What It Tolerates)
22 Juanita Way
San Francisco, California 94127
415-661-2341

This organization is action oriented, engaging in mild civil disobedience. People getting together to decide on what to do about pornography in their community is the aim of this group. Membership is welcomed and a flier on how to get involved is available.

American Library Association
Office of Intellectual Freedom
50 East Huron Street
Chicago, Illinois 60611
312-944-6780

Responsible for implementing American Library Association policies concerning intellectual freedom and free access to libraries and library materials. It is the policy of the association to oppose antipornography legislation. The office distributes information and materials. Publishes a bimonthly newsletter available to subscribers.

Citizens for Media Responsibility Without Law
P.O. Box 671
Oshkosh, Wisconsin 54902
408-427-2858

The organizers state: "Our position: We are pro-nudity and pro-sexuality. We oppose the glorification of violence in the media. We do not advocate censorship. We advocate instead community actions, short of seeking force of law, and indeed including civil disobedience, to obtain responsible publishing policies from these corporations that influence our lives." Presently the group is encouraging a boycott against any company which advertises in *Penthouse*.

D.C. Feminists Against Pornography
1519 P Street NW
Washington, D.C. 20005
202–347–5078

The purpose of D.C. Feminists Against Pornography is "to carry out an analysis of pornography as anti-woman propaganda, and to impelment an effective and fair strategy for the discouragement of pornography and other forms of sexism in sex." A newsletter, *OASIS*, is published. (Address for *OASIS* is given below.)

FACT (Feminist Anti-Censorship Taskforce)
Box 135, 660 Amsterdam Avenue
New York, New York 10025

Activities of the organization include speaking and writing on the issue of censorship of sexually explicit materials. Members of FACT have attended all the hearings held by U.S. Attorney General Meese's Commission on Pornography. FACT filed an *amicus curiae* brief in the U.S. Court of Appeals for the Seventh Circuit in April 1985, arguing that the Indianapolis antipornography ordinance should be declared unconstitutional. Copies of the brief, written by Nan Hunter and Sylvia Law, are available for $5.00 per copy. Also available are the FACT handout entitled "Why Feminists Oppose an Anti-Pornography Ordinance" and "Feminism and Censorship: Strange Bedfellows," which concisely details their reasons for opposing any form of censorship. A publication entitled *Caught Looking* appeared in 1986. People may be added to the mailing list by sending a note to the address above. FACT has chapters in other areas.

Feminists Fighting Pornography
P.O. Box 6731
Yorkville Station
New York, New York 10128
212–410–5182

An activist organization which confronts politicans, attends hearings, pickets sexist organizations, sponsors a tour of the pornography area in New York, and publishes *The Backlash Times*. The paper reports on obscenity laws and other legislation, on women victims of male violence, on examples of pornography, and on demonstrations and the other activities of this group. Members receive the newsletter and notices of meetings and demonstrations. FFP does not support obscenity laws; it does support the MacKinnon-Dworkin antipornography ordinance. Membership is $15.00.

Freedom to Read Foundation
50 East Huron Street
Chicago, Illinois 60611
312–944–6780

Promotes and protects freedom of speech and freedom of the press. Supports public right of access to libraries. Supports the right of libraries to collect and make available "any creative work they may legally acquire." Has a newsletter available to members. Volume 13, no. 1, 2–3 (1985) features article on the Indianapolis pornography ordinance and the U.S. Court of Appeals ruling.

Lesbian Herstory Archives
P.O. Box 1258
New York, New York 10016
212–874–7232

Extensive collection of material on feminists and pornography is part of this noteworthy collection. Clipping folders contain reports, articles and numerous notices, fliers, and other meeting announcements from early organizing by feminists around the issues of pornography to present-day activities. The coordinators of the collection are extremely helpful in guiding visitors and researchers through the collection.

Media Watch
1803 Mission Street, Suite 7
Santa Cruz, California 95060
408–423–4299

An activist organization which targets pornography and, through actions of civil obedience, educates the public about it. Members of the group have been arrested and make every effort to make their point in court. Media Watch welcomes participation in its activities.

National Coalition Against Censorship
132 West 43rd Street
New York, New York 10036
212–944–9899

A coalition of organizational members which takes a hard line against censorship for any reason. Individuals may subscribe to its newsletter, *Censorship News,* which frequently reports on feminist groups and the pornography issue. Most recently the coalition has been keeping track of the Meese Commission on Pornography.

New York Library Association
Intellectual Freedom Round Table
15 Park Row, Suite 434
New York, New York, 10038

The NYLA Intellectual Freedom Round Table is a membership organization that watches for infringements on intellectual freedom and particularly for attacks upon librarians and publishers. It sponsors annual programs and publishes a substantive newsletter called *Pressure Point.* Two 1985 issues of the newsletter had information on the issue of intellectual freedom and pornography and included a bibliography on the subject. The Summer 1986 issue featured several relevant news items including the text of a speech by Marcia Pally of FACT.

Pornography Awareness
P.O. Box 2728
Chapel Hill, North Carolina 27515–2728
919–967–5168

A radical feminist antipornography organization, whose purpose is to educate the community and raise consciousness about the meaning of pornography and its impact on lives and upon society. In addition to presenting numerous slide shows, the group has sponsored two symposia: "Is There a Relationship Between Pornography and Sexual Violence?" and "Women Surviving: Cultural Patterns." Group members write letters, participate in panel discussions, give lectures, and set up press conferences. Pornography Awareness shares the views of Women Against Pornography. It endorsed the Minneapolis ordinance and supports the enforcement of pandering laws and obscenity laws. Pornography Awareness is a membership organization with at least 500 members in North Carolina and the Southeast. The organization publishes information brochures and a newsletter twice a year.

Pornography Resource Center/Organizing Against Pornography
734 East Lake Street
Minneapolis, Minnesota 55407
612–822–1476

Among the objectives of this organization are to educate women, men, and children about the reality of pornography in the lives of individuals and in communities; to define and address the needs of all groups of women in relation to pornography; and to empower women to speak and act against the abuse and discrimination of pornography. The organization actively promotes education and activism around the issue of pornography. Projects include providing speakers, presenting antipornography slide shows, distributing a quarterly newsletter, supporting and planning direct action against pornographic films and advertising, collecting information on the effects of pornography, and helping others to organize locally to combat pornography. Membership is available for a fee and a bimonthly newsletter *Resource Center News* comes as part of the membership. Some of the material available: *Ordinance Packet:* The text of the Minneapolis ordinance, editorials, press coverage, information on hearings, position papers. Price: $10.00. *General Information Packet:* Contains articles on children and pornography, men and pornography, violent pornography, pornography in advertising, and racism and antisemitism in pornography. Statistics on violence against women is also included. Price: $7.50. Other materials are available including the transcript of the public hearing in Minneapolis (December 1984), for $40.00.

Progressive Action Against Media Abuse
P.O. Box 18777
Denver, Colorado 80218
303–320–0304

Progressive Action Against Media Abuse is a "prosex" feminist organization dedicated to eradicating oppressive media messages and imagery. Through community education programs and activism it works against the media propagation of sexism, racism, heterosexism, classism, exploitation of children, and glorification of violence—especially in advertising, film, radio, video, and television. They support media portrayals which humanize rather than objectify people. Contributions are welcome. A newsletter, *The Activist*, contains articles, editorials, book reviews, news items, commentary, and meeting schedules. The July 1986 issue contained a lengthy editorial titled "The Meese Commission—Coopting Our Issues for Rightest Repression?"

Task Force on Pornography and Prostitution
P.O. Box 1602
Madison, Wisconsin 53701

The role of this organization has been largely educational; they sponsored a symposium by Catharine MacKinnon, Edward Donnerstein, and others. The group's stance is antipornography, although it seems interested in fostering public discussion of all issues.

Women Against Pornography
1214 Ridgecrest
Monterey Park, California 91754
213–269–3097

This group was formed to work for the proposed Los Angeles County Pornography Civil Rights Ordinance. The group is not now active, but questions about their organizing, their activities, and their experiences will be answered.

Women Against Pornography
358 W. 47th Street
New York, New York 10036
212-307–5055

WAP has weekly discussion meetings on various issues related to women and pornography. A recent calendar listed consciousness-raising groups, programs on "Lesbian pornography," civil rights antipornography update, international female sexual slavery discussion, and women and AIDS. They sponsor feminist-guided tours of the Times Square pornography district and present slide shows on such topics as "Pornography, Sexual Abuse, and Inequality," "Sex

Roles for Sale," "Roles in Rock," "Disability," "Sexism in Advertising," and "Pornography and Racism." They also have prepared resource booklets containing information sources, statistics, and action plans. Women Against Pornography have a ninety-minute presentation and slide show which has been made available to many groups. Various categories of membership are available from $15.00 to $500.

Appendix A

A Short List of Publications Which Contain Frequent References to the Feminist Antipornography Movement

These publications contain news items, letters to the editor, and other references in almost every issue examined, some items too brief to warrant a whole entry in this bibliography. These titles are listed for those who want to examine all letters, commentaries, and brief news reports written. A few are included, with addresses, because they are hard to locate.

Aegis: Magazine on Ending Violence Against Women
Quarterly publication for sharing ideas among women organizing against rape, battering, harassment, and other forms of violence against women.
P.O. Box 21033
Washington, D.C. 20009

The Backlash Times
Sixteen-page magazine published quarterly by Feminists Fighting Pornography. International news on pornography, sexism, violence against women and women fighting back.
P.O. Box 6731
Yorkville Station
New York, New York, 10128

The Body Politic
A monthly magazine for lesbians and gay men published in Canada. Includes news, reviews of books and films, and feature articles. Frequently mentions antipornography issues, especially in Canada.
Indexed in the *Alternative Press Index*.
Pink Triangle Press, Box 639, Station A
Toronto, Ontario M5W1G2, Canada

Feminist Periodicals: A Current Listing of Contents
Published on a quarterly basis. Helpful to perusing the table of
contents pages reproduced from many feminist periodicals. There is
also a separate listing of all titles covered with complete bibliographic data, ordering information, and where indexed.
Women's Studies Librarian-at-Large
University of Wisconsin System
112A Memorial Library
728 State Street
Madison, Wisconsin 53706

Gay Community News
A weekly publication produced by a collective in Boston which
covers "events and news in the interest of gay and lesbian liberation."
The "News Notes" page includes national and international items.
Many books reviews.
Indexed in the *Alternative Press Index*
167 Tremont Street
Boston, Massachusetts 02111

Harvard Women's Law Journal
A publication devoted to the development of a feminist jurispru-
dence and to the presentation of women's legal issues.
Hastings Hall
Harvard Law School
Cambridge, Massachusetts 02138

Lesbian Herstory Archives Newsletter
An occasional report of Archives happenings—including a bibliogra-
phy on some aspect of Lesbian Culture, new acquisitions, research
queries, discoveries, and announcements.
P.O. Box 1258
New York, New York, 10116

Media Report to Women
The subtitle of this bimonthly publication is "What women are
doing and thinking to build more democratic communication systems." It gives summaries of selected quotations from articles on all

aspects of communication. Frequently covers the pornography-censorship-feminist issue.

3306 Ross Place N.W.
Washington, D.C. 20008

New Directions For Women
"A national feminist periodical written for feminists and committed to reaching out to those not yet dedicated to a feminist future." Extensive letters and commentary space. Many news items and articles about the antipornography movement. Bimonthly.

108 W. Palisade Avenue
Englewood, New Jersey 07631

OASIS (Organized Against Sexism in Sex)
Newsletter of D.C. Feminists Against Pornography, an activist/educational organization protesting sexism and violence against women in the community, pornography, and mass media.

P.O. Box 33947
Farragut Station
Washington, D.C. 20033

Off Our Backs
International and national news; features articles including regular reporting on work, health, prison, education, and lesbian issues; reviews; letters. Coverage of conferences, actions, policies and theory. Eleven issues per year. Indexed in *Women's Studies Abstracts; Alternative Press Index; New Periodical Index.*

1841 Columbia Road, NW, Room 212
Washington, D.C. 20009

Pornography Resource Center News
News on organizing against pornography, locally and nationally; current research, actions, opinions, and analysis covering child pornography, legal issues, and information on the pornography industry.

Pornography Resource Center
734 E. Lake Street, 3d Floor
Minneapolis, Minnesota 55407

Sojourner
National monthly that provides open forum for women. Features
and invites essays; interviews; book, film, and music reviews; poetry;
fiction; notices; letters.
143 Albany Street
Cambridge, Massachusetts 02139

Womanews (New York City)
A New York City feminist newspaper and calendar of events. Every
issue examined, or very nearly so, contained an article or a news
report or a letter to the editor on the controversy concerning
feminists and pornography.
P.O. Box 220, Village Station
New York, New York, 10014

Women Against Pornography Newsreport
Devoted to informing women and men about activities, legal development and events pertaining to violence and pornography against
women.
358 W. 47th St.
New York, New York, 10036

Women Against Sexist Violence in Pornography and Media
Organizes tours of the pornography district in Pittsburgh and makes
recommendations for action against pornographic films. Their newsletter includes reports on demonstrations, film and other media, and
relevant news from elsewhere in the country.
P.O. Box 7172
Pittsburgh, Pennsylvania 15213

Women's Alliance Against Pornography
This organization was responsible for collecting over 5,000 signatures needed to place the referendum question on pornography on
the Cambridge ballot in November 1985, and to force the Cambridge City Council, via a law suit, to put the issue on the ballot.
Members of WAAP were particularly active at this time in working
with local women who had been harmed by pornography and were
ready to use the legislation. WAAP continues to work as both an
educational and activist organization working with other organiza-

tions nationwide to raise consciousness on the effects of pornography on all women.

P.O. Box 2027
Cambridge, Massachusetts 02238

The Women's Review of Books
In-depth reviews of current books by and/or about women, published monthly.

Wellesley Center for Research on Women
Wellesley, Massachusetts 02181

Appendix B

Newspapers: A Chronology

This chronology of newspaper articles includes only the daily newspapers. Please refer to the newspaper section of this bibliography for the annotation.

1976

1 April 1976
Maddocks, Melvin. " 'Snuff' and Liberal Conscience." *Christian Science Monitor, 30.*

1977

21 July 1977
"Feminists vs. Pornography." *Christian Science Monitor, 28.*
16 August 1977
Cohen, Richard. "Issues Often Viewed Through Special Lens." *Washington Post,* sec. C, 1.

1978

26 January 1978
Jacoby, Susan. "Hers." *New York Times,* sec. C, 2.
24 March 1978
Morgan, Robin. "Check It Out: Porn, No. But Free Speech, Yes." *New York Times, 27.*
4 December 1978
Klemesrud, Judy. "Women, Pornography, Free Speech: A Fierce Debate at N. Y. U." *New York Times,* sec. D, 10.
24 December 1978
"How Not to Fight Pornography." *New York Times,* sec. D, 10.

1979

9 February 1979
Dershowitz, Alan M. "Free-Free-Speech." *New York Times, 31.*
6 July 1979
Dullea, Georgia. "In Feminists' Antipornography Drive, 42nd Street Is the Target." *New York Times,* sec. A, 12.

1979 *(cont.)*

17 September 1979

Bennetts, Leslie. "Conference Examines Pornography As A Feminist Issue." *New York Times,* sec. B, 10.

2 October 1979

Terp, Christine. "Women Against Pornography." *Christian Science Monitor,* sec. B, 8.

21 October 1979

Basler, Barbara. "5,000 Join Feminist Group's Rally in Times Square Against Pornography." *New York Times,* sec. A, 41.

1980

18 May 1980

Cohen, Richard. "Star of 'Deep Throat' Reveals a Lot About Porn." *Washington Post,* sec. C, 1.

3 August 1980

Ennis, Kathleen. "Feminists Take Protests to 14th Street." *Washington Post,* sec. B, 7.

Feshbach, Seymour. "Mixing Sex With Violence—A Dangerous Alchemy." *New York Times,* sec. D, 29.

1981

9 February 1981

Serrin, William. "Sex is a Multibillion Business in U.S. and Expanding." *New York Times,* sec. B, 1.

10 February 1981

Serrin, William. "Opponents of Flourishing Sex Industry Hindered by Its Open Public Acceptance." *New York Times,* sec. B, 6.

3 March 1981

Klemesrud, Judy. " 'Lolita Syndrome' Is Denounced." *New York Times,* sec. B, 14.

19 May 1981

Goodman, Ellen. "Protecting Free Speech *And* Our Children." *Washington Post,* sec. A, 13.

Hentoff, Nat. "The Lust to Censor." *Washington Post,* sec. A, 13.

26 May 1981

Dworkin, Andrea. "Pornography's Part in Sexual Violence." *Los Angeles Times,* sec. 2, 5.

27 September 1981

1981 *(cont.)*
Weil, Martin, and Peter Eng. "Women March Against Pornography." *Washington Post*, sec. B, 8.
6 October 1981
Irwin, Victoria. "A Conflict of Images; Fashion Magazines: What Do They Say About Women?" *Christian Science Monitor*, 18, midwestern ed.
12 October 1981
Suplee, Curt, and James Lardner. "Writers of the World, Unite!: Congress of Authors Assaults 'Literary Industrial Complex.' " *Washington Post*, sec. D, 1, 3.

1982
11 February 1982
"Personalities." *Washington Post*, sec. D, 2.

1983
18 December 1983
"Minneapolis Asked to Attack Pornography As Rights Issue." *New York Times*, sec. A, part 1, 44.
31 December 1983
Wehrwein, Austin C. "Smut Is Declared Illegal Sex Bias In Minneapolis." *Washington Post*, sec. A, 3.

1984
4 January 1984
"Pornography: A Civil Rights Issue?" *Washington Post*, sec. A, 16.
6 January 1984
Japenga, Ann. "Sex-Violence Research: He Takes a Feminist Approach." *Los Angeles Times*, sec. 5, 1, 14.
"Minneapolis Mayor Vetoes Plan Defining Pornography as Sex Bias." *New York Times*, sec. A, 11.
Wehrwein, Austin. "Mayor Vetoes Ordinance in Minneapolis Labeling Pornography Sex Bias." *Washington Post*, sec. A, 2.
8 January 1984
Will, George F. " 'Rights' vs. Smut in Minneapolis." *Washington Post*, sec. C, 7.
9 January 1984
Yardley, Jonathan. "The Porn Predicament: It's Not Being Prudish to Want To Stop the Sleaze." *Washington Post*, sec. B, 1.

1984 *(cont.)*

12 January 1984

Sitomer, Curtis J. "A Nationwide Boycott of Pornography Might Do What the Courts Can't." *Christian Science Monitor,* 19.

14 January 1984

Goodman, Ellen. "Pornography Is Harmful, But. . . ." *Washington Post,* sec. A, 21.

8 February 1984

Michaelson, Judith. "Sexual Violence and the Media." *Los Angeles Times,* sec. 6, 1, 8.

4 March 1984

Holt, Joyce Sunila. "DePalma's Rage to Sow a Porn Plot." *Los Angeles Times,* Calendar, 37.

5 April 1984

Buchwald, Art. "First Amendment's Passionate Protector." *Los Angeles Times,* sec. 5, 3.

10 April 1984

"Measure Seeks to Curb Violent Pornography." *New York Times,* sec. A, 22.

24 April 1984

"Indianapolis Approves Antipornography Law." *New York Times,* sec. A, 17.

12 May 1984

"Indiana Porn." *Washington Post,* sec. A, 14.

15 May 1984

Shipp, E. R. "Civil Rights Law Against Pornography Is Challenged." *New York Times,* sec. A, 14.

23 May 1984

Low, Charlotte. "Feminism Clashes With Civil Liberties Over Pornography." *Los Angeles Times,* sec. 2, 7.

27 May 1984

"Censorship Is No One's Civil Right." *New York Times,* sec. D, 16.

10 June 1984

Shipp, E. R. "A Feminist Offensive Against Exploitation." *New York Times,* sec. D, 2.

17 June 1984

Osterman, Steven D. "The Censor's Pen Is Not Women's Best Protection; the Problem of Obscenity Cannot Be Solved by Doing Violence to the First Amendment." *Los Angeles Times,* sec. 4, 5.

1984 *(cont.)*

3 July 1984
Goldstein, Al. "Cable TV's Shame: 'Gore-nography.' " *New York Times,* sec. A, 15.
Goodman, Walter. "Battle on Pornography Spurred by New Tactics." *New York Times,* sec. A, 8.
14 July 1984
"Demonstration Hits Decision on Obscenity Law." *Washington Post,* sec. A, 6.
"Protesters Press Pornography Law: 20 Are Arrested in Minneapolis In Bid Against City Council Delay On an Ordinance." *New York Times,* 8, 46.
29 July 1984
Kurtz, Howard. "New War on Pornography, Librarians Argue With Preachers Over City Law." *Washington Post,* sec. A, 4.
31 July 1984
Shipp, E. R. "Federal Judge Hears Arguments on Validity of Indianapolis Pornography Measure." *New York Times,* sec. A, 10.
3 August 1984
"Censors in White Robes." *Los Angeles Times,* sec. 2, 4.
Sitomer, Curtis J. "Censorship, the Spirit and the Letter." *Christian Science Monitor,* sec. B, 6.
13 August 1984
Goodman, Walter. "Pornography: Esthetics to Censorship Debated." *New York Times,* sec. C, 21.
16 August 1984
"Council Panel Studies Tough Anti-Porn Law." *Los Angeles Times,* sec. 1, 21.
31 August 1984
Hentoff, Nat. "War on Pornography: The First Casualty is Free Speech." *Washington Post,* sec. A, 21.
10 September 1984
"Censorship and Pornography." *Los Angeles Times,* sec. 2, 4.
26 September 1984
Duggan, Lisa, and Ann Snitow. "Porn Law Is About Images, Not Power." *Newsday* (New York), 65.
7 October 1984
Rather, John. "Pornography Bill Stirs Furor in Suffolk." *New York Times,* sec. 11LI, 1.

1984 *(cont.)*

13 November 1984

Gruson, Lindsey. "Pornography Bill is Issue in Suffolk." *New York Times,* sec. B, 2.

19 November 1984

"Censors in Feminist Garb." *New York Times,* sec. A, 22.

21 November 1984

"Debate Persists on Rights and Smut." *New York Times,* sec. A, 17.

22 November 1984

"Points of View: Of Censorship." *New York Times,* sec. A, 26.

24 November 1984

Headden, Susan. "Judge Tosses Out City's Porn Law." *Indianapolis Star,* 1.

25 November 1984

"Censors Fail to See the Danger." *Los Angeles Times,* sec. 4, 4.

29 November 1984

Hentoff, Nat. "A Hoosier Madisonian." *Washington Post,* sec. A, 27.

27 December 1984

"Suffolk Officials Vote Down Bill on Pornography." *New York Times,* sec. B, 5.

31 December 1984

Oliver, Myrna. "Indianapolis Dispute on Porn Law Disturbs Calm of Staid, 'Clean' City." *Los Angeles Times,* sec. 1, 8.

1985

13 January 1985

Lewis, Stephen. "Long Island Opinion: Pornography and the Issues Facing Suffolk." *New York Times,* sec. 11LI, 18.

27 February 1985

Connell, Rich. "County to Explore Adoption of Tough Pornography Law." *Los Angeles Times,* sec. 2, 1, 3.

28 February 1985

"The Censors Among Us." *Los Angeles Times,* sec. 2, 4.

16 March 1985

Decker, Cathleen. "Feminists Resist Pornography Law." *Los Angeles Times,* sec. 2, 1.

21 March 1985

Hunter, Nan D. "Anti-Pornography Measure Could Backfire on Women." *Los Angeles Times,* sec. 2, 5.

1985 *(cont.)*

25 March 1985

Karkabi, Barbara. "Seminar Addresses Pornography." *Houston Chronicle,* sec. 5, 2.

27 March 1985

Connell, Rich. "Showdown on County Anti-Smut Law Put Off." *Los Angeles Times,* sec. 2, 3.

21 May 1985

Shenon, Philip. "Meese Named Panel to Study How to Control Pornography." *New York Times,* sec. A. 21.

28 May 1985

Stevenson, Gail. "Tolerance of Porn Traumatizes Women." *Los Angeles Times,* sec. 2, 5.

1 June 1985

Savage, David G. "Violence and Women: Researchers Condemn R-Rated Films as Worse Offenders Than Pornographic Movies." *Los Angeles Times,* sec. 2, 1, 6.

2 June 1985

Mancusi, Peter. "Free to Express—Or Suppress?" *Boston Globe,* sec. A, 17.

4 June 1985

Vollmer, Ted. "Counsel Urges Compromise in Pornography Law." *Los Angeles Times,* sec. 2, 1, 6.

5 June 1985

Vollmer, Ted. "County Rejects Wide Anti-Smut Law; 2 Weaker Ones Okd." *Los Angeles Times,* sec. 2, 1, 6.

14 June 1985

Klemesrud, Judy. "Bill on Pornography Opposed." *New York Times,* sec. A, 18.

21 June 1985

Clifford, Frank. "Disputed Anti-Porn Measure Faces Council Test." *Los Angeles Times,* sec. 2, 1, 6.

"FBI Director Is Content With Antismut Arsenal." *Washington Post,* sec. A, 16.

22 June 1985

Clifford, Frank. "Council Rejects Anti-Pornography Law." *Los Angeles Times,* sec. 2, 1, 3.

23 June 1985

"Is New Action Needed on Pornography?" *New York Times,* sec. D, 24.

1985 *(cont.)*

11 July 1985
Sitomer, Curtis J. "Sifting Out Pornography From Free Speech." *Christian Science Monitor,* 21.
14 July 1985
Lederer, Laura. "Pornography: Think About It." *San Francisco Chronicle,* This World Section, 20.
24 July 1985
Shannon, William V. "The Pornography Evil." *Boston Globe,* 15.
26 August 1985
Klemesrud, Judy. "Joining Hands in the Fight Against Pornography." *New York Times,* sec. B, 7.
28 August 1985
"U.S. Court Rejects an Anti-Smut Law." *New York Times,* sec. A, 21.
1 September 1985
Duggan, Lisa. "The Dubious Porn War Alliance." *Washington Post,* sec. C, 1, 4.
8 September 1985
Gardner, Sandra. "New Jerseyans." *New York Times,* sec. 11NJ, 6.
11 September 1985
Hirshson, Paul. "Council Vote Blocks Ballot Question on Pornography in Cambridge." *Boston Globe,* 24.
14 September 1985
Hentoff, Nat. "Civil-Rights Censors." *Washington Post,* sec. A, 19.
15 September 1985
Clines, Francis S. "A Tale of Two Views on Erotica." *New York Times,* sec. A, part 2, 62.
3 October 1985
"SJC Orders Cambridge to Put Antiporn Referendum on Ballot." *Boston Globe,* 18.
6 October 1985
Hirshson, Paul. "Pornography Fighter Backs Cambridge Plan." *Boston Globe,* 42.
9 October 1985
Lederer, Laura J. "Pornography Is a Social Carcinogen." *Los Angeles Times,* sec. 2, 5.
15 October 1985
Kurtz, Howard. "Pornography Panel's Objectivity Disputed: Critics Call Meese Commission Overzealous." *Washington Post,* sec. A, 4.

1985 *(cont.)*

1 November 1985
Lindsay, Leon. "Proposed Law Would Make Pornography a Human-Rights Issue." *Christian Science Monitor,* 6.
9 November 1985
Hirshson, Paul. "Antipornography Vote Appears Headed for Defeat in Cambridge." *Boston Globe,* 23.
10 November 1985
Hirshson, Paul. "Antismut Law Looks Dead in Cambridge." *Boston Globe,* 33, 37.
12 November 1985
Hirshson, Paul. "Cambridge Ends Counting; 4 New Officials." *Boston Globe,* 45.

1986

25 February 1986
Carelli, Richard. "Supreme Court Rejects Pornography Ordinance." *Boston Globe,* 3.
"A Greater Harm." *Los Angeles Times,* sec. 2, 4.
Hager, Philip. "Court Voids Law on Pornography." *Los Angeles Times,* sec. 1, 10.
Jackman, Frank. "Justices XXX Out a Sex Law." *Daily News* (New York), 7.
Taylor, Stuart, Jr. "Pornography Foes Lose New Weapon in Supreme Court." *New York Times,* sec. A, 1, 26.
26 February 1986
Taylor, Stuart, Jr. "High Court Backs Use of Zoning to Regulate Showing of Sex Films." *New York Times,* sec. A, 1, 20.
28 February 1986
"Putting Porno In Its Place." *Wall Street Journal,* 24, eastern ed.
14 April 1986
Blumenthal, Karen. "Adult-Magazine Ban Brings Cries of Censorship." *Wall Street Journal,* 31, eastern ed.
14 May 1986
Sitomer, Curtis J. "Panel Sees Porn as Civil Rights Issue." *Christian Science Monitor,* 1, 6, 7.
17 May 1986
Goleman, Daniel. "Researchers Dispute Pornography Report On Its Use of Data." *New York Times,* sec. A, 1, 35.

1986 *(cont.)*

27 May 1986
"Detailed Descriptions in Pornography Report." *New York Times,*
sec. A, 17.
2 June 1986
"Defeated by Pornography." *New York Times,* sec. A, 16.
12 June 1986
Wald, Matthew L. "Maine Anti-Obscenity Plan Soundly Defeated."
New York Times, sec. A, 27.
10 July 1986
"Excerpts From Final Report of Attorney General's Panel on Por-
nography." *New York Times,* sec. B, 7.
Gamarekian, Barbara. "Report Draws Strong Praise and Criticism."
New York Times, sec. B, 7.
Pear, Robert. "Panel Calls on Citizens to Wage National Assault on
Pornography." *New York Times,* sec. A, 1, Sec. B, 7.
13 July 1986
"Final Report on Pornography Prompts Debate." *New York Times,*
sec. E, 4.
"The Story of X." *New York Times,* sec. E, 28.
3 August 1986
Martin, Douglas. "Canada vs. Pornography: Even *Playboy* May Fall."
sec. A, 4.
5 October 1986
Kristof, Nicholas D. "X-Rated Industry in a Slump." *New York
Times,* sec. 3, 1, 6.

Index